Catholic Shrines and Places of Pilgrimage in the United States

Office for the Pastoral Care of Migrants and Refugees
United States Catholic Conference

In March 1989, the Bishops' Committee on Migration authorized the preparation of a Catholic directory of shrines and places of pilgrimage in the United States. The Office for the Pastoral Care of Migrants and Refugees was commissioned to prepare this publication for the promotion of the shrine and pilgrimage apostolate. This directory, *Catholic Shrines and Places of Pilgrimage in the United States,* has been reviewed by Most Rev. James P. Keleher, the Episcopal Liaison for the Shrine and Pilgrimage Apostolate. It is hereby authorized for publication by the undersigned.

Monsignor Robert N. Lynch
General Secretary
NCCB/USCC

May 18, 1992

Cover by Niki Pino/ABNC Design

ISBN 1-55586-517-8

Contents

NORTHEAST   41

New Hampshire

New Jersey

New York

Pennsylvania

Rhode Island

Vermont

SOUTH   85

Kentucky

Louisiana

Oklahoma

Tennessee

Texas

SOUTHEAST   105

Delaware

WEST   121

Alphabetical Listing of Shrines (Using Proper Titles)   141

Shrines and Places Dedicated to the Mystery of Christ   144

Shrines and Places Dedicated to the Blessed Mother   145

Shrines and Places Dedicated to the Saints   147

Introduction

Rev. Anthony Czarnecki
USCC Liaison for the Shrine and Pilgrimage Apostolate

This Shrine Directory is being offered in response to many requests from those interested in the shrine and pilgrimage apostolate in the United States. The data on the shrines were obtained from a survey conducted by the Office for the Pastoral Care of Migrants and Refugees. A brief historical profile is presented for each shrine, together with schedules of devotions, various pastoral services, and social activities.

In our research we concentrated our efforts on the sites that reflect the Church's definition of a shrine as stated in the *New Code of Canon Law:* ". . . a shrine signifies a Church or other sacred place to which the faithful make pilgrimages for a particular pious reason, with the approval of the local ordinary" (c1230). Thus, this publication is not intended to provide a complete listing of all the places of pilgrimage in the United States.

The emerging interest in pilgrimage makes this directory a very timely response to the needs of people. In this often impersonal and technological world, people who seek spiritual experiences are turning to the shrines as centers where they can regain peace of mind and heart, a place where they can experience the Divine in the midst of their daily lives. Over centuries of Christian tradition, many basilicas, medieval shrines, grottoes, churches, and monuments have been built and developed. These shrines are vivid manifestations of the faith, beliefs, and cultural attitudes of both individuals and communities passing through generations. In 1992, during the First World Congress on Shrines and Pilgrimages sponsored by the Pontifical Council on Migrants and Itinerant People, Archbishop Giovanni Cheli stated, "Shrines, whether big or small, are earthly images of the Eternal Shrine . . . where God speaks to whomever will listen."

In our country, we are witnessing a significant growth in the pilgrimage movement, and also an increase of religious tourists who seek a new experience at holy sites during their vacation time or on business travel. Many shrine directors are aware of contemporary pilgrims' needs and are responding with a variety of pastoral services such as healing services, prayer ministry, liturgical and paraliturgical devotions, and cultural programs. The Episcopal Liaison for the Shrine and Pilgrimage Apostolate of the United States Catholic Conference, Most Rev. James P. Keleher, together with the National Association of Shrines and Diocesan Directors on Pilgrimage fosters this emerging movement and reflects on its meaning in the mission of the Church.

Various rituals, acts of worship, and artistic expressions developed in the shrines have become the means of personal contact with God for pilgrims. Religion, like life itself, needs warmth, emotion, celebration, and inspiration. People find these values in shrines and continue to search for them on pilgrimage to many contemporary sacred sites in the United States and throughout the world. We hope that this directory will provide suitable information for people interested in the shrine and pilgrimage apostolate.

NORTH DAKOTA

MINNESOTA

SOUTH DAKOTA

WISCONSIN

MICHIGAN

NEBRASKA

IOWA

ILLINOIS

INDIANA

OHIO

KANSAS

MISSOURI

MIDWEST

NATIONAL SHRINE OF OUR LADY OF THE SNOWS

9500 W. Illinois Route 15, Belleville, Ill. 62223
(618) 397-6700 or (314) 241-3400

History of the Shrine:

In 1818, Blessed Eugene DeMazenod, the founder of the Missionary Oblates of Mary Immaculate, accepted the care and ministry of the Shrine of Notre Dame de Laus in France for his newly established group of missionaries. Thus, Oblates have been linked to shrine ministry from the time of their founding.

In 1941, Fr. Paul Schulte, OMI, a missionary in the Arctic regions of Canada, first introduced devotion to Mary under the title of Our Lady of Snows to those in the Midwest. Devotion to Mary under this title has ties to the legend about a snowfall that occurred in Rome in 352 A.D. after Mary had appeared in a dream to a Roman couple. It was Fr. Edwin J. Guild, OMI, who actually founded this largest outdoor shrine in the country dedicated to Mary as Our Lady of the Snows.

The many attractions at the shrine include the Way of the Cross, an outdoor altar and 3,500-seat amphitheater, Lourdes Grotto, Christ's Agony in the Garden, Resurrection Garden, Annunciation Garden, Edwin J. Guild Center, Christ the King Chapel, and the Mary Chapel.

The shrine is open every day of the year to people of all faiths and denominations. Activities during the year include an American Indian celebration (July 11-18), Annual Celebration of Our Lady of Snows (July 31-August 2), Polish-American Celebration (August 15), World Youth Day (October 25), and the 23rd Annual Way of Lights (November 27-January 3).

Schedule of Masses:

Sunday Vigil: 5:00 p.m.
Sunday: 9:30 a.m. and 11:30 a.m.
Daily: April-October: 7:30 a.m., 11:30 a.m., and 5:00 p.m.;
November-March: 7:30 a.m. and 11:30 a.m.
Confessions: Thirty minutes before each Mass

Devotions:

Rosary: Monday-Friday: 8:45 a.m., Lourdes Grotto; Saturday: 8:30 p.m.

Facilities:

Visitors Center
Gift Shop
Restaurant
Overnight Accommodations (Pilgrims Inn Motel)

DOMINICAN SHRINE OF ST. JUDE THADDEUS

1909 South Ashland Avenue, Chicago, Ill. 60608
(312) 226-0020

**History
of the
Shrine:** The Dominican Shrine of St. Jude Thaddeus, opened in October 1929, encompasses a ministry of preaching, spiritual direction, and a network of people at prayer, The Friends of St. Jude. The Friends of St. Jude write, telephone, and stop at the shrine to request prayers for their special needs. The shrine, in the parish church of St. Pius V, is staffed by the Dominican Fathers and Brothers of the Province of St. Albert the Great.

**Schedule
of Masses:** Sunday Parish Masses: 8:00 a.m. and 11:15 a.m. (English); 9:30 a.m., 1:00 p.m., and 4:30 p.m. (Spanish)
Holy Day of Obligation: 8:00 a.m. (parish), 12:00 p.m. (shrine service)
Confessions: Saturday: 5:00 p.m.; Thursday and each novena day: 12:00 p.m. and 6:25 p.m.

Devotions: Rosary, novena prayers, and eucharist each day (except Sunday) at 12:00 p.m. and Thursday at 6:30 p.m. Solemn novenas are held five times a year (January, March, May, July, and October), with services at 9:50 a.m., 12:00 p.m., and 6:30 p.m. (also Sunday at 11:00 a.m.).

Facilities: Gift Shop

NATIONAL SHRINE OF ST. ANNE

38th Place and California Avenue, Chicago, Ill. 60632
(312) 927-2421

History of the Shrine:

In 1662, Fr. Morel, pastor of the parish church in Beaupre, Canada, wrote a letter to Bishop de Lavel in which he exclaimed, "Of much more importance than all these cures are the spiritual graces daily bestowed by Almighty God through the intercession of good St. Anne on many . . . by converting him/her to a better life."

Because of the many spiritual favors and miracles of grace, the Shrine of St. Anne of Brighton has become one of the largest and most significant shrines in the country. Thousands of pilgrims, unable to visit the original shrine of St. Anne de Beaupre, continue to come here.

An annual novena is offered to St. Anne, most recently during July 18-26, 1991. Those who wish to join the Archconfraternity of St. Anne are invited to do so. Throughout the year, from the eighteenth to the twenty-sixth of each month, a novena of Masses is offered for those enrolled in the Archconfraternity.

Schedule of Masses:

During Novena Week
Daily: 6:30 a.m., 8:00 a.m., and 9:30 a.m.
Novena Mass: Weekdays, 9:30 a.m.; Sunday, 9:00 a.m.
Confessions: Before the 9:30 a.m. Mass and after all novena services

Devotions:

During Novena Week
Morning Prayers: Daily: After 9:30 a.m. Mass
Afternoon Novena Service: Daily: 2:00 p.m.
Evening Novena Services: Daily: 6:30 and 8:00 p.m.
Blessing for Children: Saturday: 2:00 p.m.
Blessing for the Sick: Sunday: 2:00 p.m. and 4:00 p.m.
Outdoor Procession: July 20 and 23: After the 8:00 p.m. service; also July 26 (Feast of St. Anne)
Veneration of the Relic

Facilities:

Cafeteria
Religious Goods Store

NATIONAL SHRINE OF ST. JUDE

205 West Monroe Street, Chicago, Ill. 60606 (312) 236-7782

History of the Shrine:

Devotion to St. Jude, one of the Twelve Apostles and a cousin of Jesus, was slow to develop, perhaps due to confusion of his name with that of Judas Iscariot. Impetus to this devotion was given by the Lord himself who, in a vision, directed St. Bridget of Sweden to turn to St. Jude with faith and confidence.

The first widespread public veneration of St. Jude in the western hemisphere took place in 1911 in Chile at a large shrine to the Apostle built by the Claretian Missionary Fathers. In the United States, the first major shrine to the apostle was established in 1929 in Chicago, also by the Claretian Missionary Fathers. The National Shrine of St. Jude contains the largest first-class relic of the saint in North America.

Fr. James Tort, CMF, during the Great Depression, began a Novena to St. Jude, the patron saint of difficult or hopeless cases, on February 17, 1929. The congregation responded enthusiastically and spread the word of the devotions across the nation. Over the years, many other shrines and publications devoted to St. Jude have come into being. He is a model of Christ's disciples to all who honor him.

The shrine has received more than one million letters of thanks for favors granted through the intercession of St. Jude. The shrine is open to the public 7:00 a.m.-8:00 p.m. daily.

Schedule of Masses:

Weekday: 8:15 a.m. (English), 7:00 a.m. and 7:00 p.m. (Spanish)
Sunday Vigil: 7:00 p.m.
Sunday: 10:30 a.m. and 4:30 p.m. (English); 7:30 a.m., 9:00 a.m., 11:45 a.m., 1:15 p.m. and 6:00 p.m. (Spanish)
Holy Day of Obligation: 8:15 a.m. and 4:30 p.m. (English); 7:00 a.m. and 7:00 p.m. (Spanish)
Confessions: Saturday: 3:00-5:00 p.m. and 6:00-7:00 p.m.

Devotions:

St. Jude: Wednesday: 5:30 p.m. and 8:00 p.m.
Solemn Novenas to St. Jude: February (preceding Lent), April (preceding Mother's Day), June (preceding Father's Day), August, and October (Feast of St. Jude)
Solemn Novena Services: Monday-Saturday: 2:00 p.m., 5:30 p.m., and 8:00 p.m.; Sunday: 3:00 p.m. and 8:00 p.m.

Facilities: Gift Shop

Languages: English and Spanish

OUR LADY OF SORROWS BASILICA AND NATIONAL SHRINE

3121 W. Jackson Boulevard, Chicago, Ill. 60612
(312) 638-5800

History of the Shrine:

The establishment of this shrine is associated with the Servite Order. The Servite Order (for Servants of Mary) was founded in 1233 by seven young merchants in Florence, Italy and was spread throughout the world under the patronage of Our Lady of Sorrows. It is thought by many that the order was founded by Mary — she is portrayed on the east transept altar speaking to the founders, all of whom have been canonized by the Church.

The idea for an Our Lady of Sorrows parish came from two Servite Fathers who were conducting a mission at Old St. Patrick's Church in Chicago in 1874. They acted quickly, and by Christmas of that year, Our Lady of Sorrows National Shrine was founded as a parish. A larger church was dedicated on January 5, 1902, was consecrated in 1956, and was named a basilica by Pope Pius XII in 1957.

The basilica seats about twelve hundred people and has a main altar, two major altars in the transepts, and ten small chapels, including the Chapel of Our Lady of Fatima, the Sacred Heart Chapel, the Chapel of St. Therese of Lisieux, St. Anne's Chapel, the Pieta Chapel, and the Friars Chapel. Surrounding the sanctuary are a majestic sacristy, a relic chapel with beautiful woodwork and stained glass, and a shrine featuring a full-sized marble replica of Michelangelo's *Pieta*.

The basilica and shrine are open Monday-Saturday, 8:15 a.m.-5:00 p.m. and Sunday, 9:30 a.m.-12:00 p.m.

Schedule of Masses:

Weekdays: Monday-Saturday: 8:30 a.m.
Sunday: 10:30 a.m.
Holy Day of Obligation: 8:30 a.m.
Confessions: Available during pilgrimages and Lent and upon request

Devotions:

Sorrowful Mother Novena: Fridays: 8:00 a.m. and 5:00 p.m.
Special Liturgies, Novenas, or Stations of the Cross may be arranged for pilgrimage groups.
Our Lady of Sorrows Festival: September 15

Facilities:

Gift Shop
Parish Hall
Hospitality Room
Museum

ST. FRANCES X. CABRINI CHAPEL AND NATIONAL SHRINE

c/o Columbus Hospital, 2520 North Lakeview Avenue, Chicago, Ill. 60614 (312) 883-6400

History of the Shrine:

The shrine is located on the shores of Lake Michigan in the Columbus Hospital. The hospital continues its mission of health care in the spirit of its foundress, St. Frances Xavier Cabrini. At the request of Archbishop Quigley of Chicago, Reverend Mother Frances X. Cabrini of the Missionary Sisters of the Sacred Heart established Columbus Hospital on February 25, 1905. It was expanded first in 1920 and, subsequently, in 1950 and 1958.

The south wing of the hospital, adjacent to the St. Frances X. Cabrini Chapel, contains rooms in which our first American citizen saint lived while in Chicago. It is there that she died on December 22, 1917. Mother Cabrini was canonized in 1946. The shrine has been restored to its original simplicity for the benefit of those thousands of visitors who come seeking peace, comfort, and consolation.

The major celebrations of the year are the Feast of St. Frances X. Cabrini on November 13 and the Feast of the Sacred Heart in June.

Schedule of Masses:

Sunday Vigil: 4:00 p.m.
Sunday: 10:00 a.m.
Daily: Two Masses are celebrated
Holy Day of Obligation: 10:00 a.m.
Confessions: Upon request

Devotions:

Novenas: Weekly
Services for employees and patients are held in the hospital chapel.

Facilities:

Religious Bookstore
Gift Shop
Access to Pastoral Care Staff of the hospital

Languages:

English, Spanish, and Italian

NATIONAL SHRINE OF ST. THERESE

8501 Bailey Road, Darien, Ill. 60559 (312) 969-5050

History of the Shrine:

The shrine, situated on fifty acres of land at the intersection of Interstate 55 and Cass Avenue, is staffed by the Carmelites, who have been in the area for the past 31 years. This new shrine was established recently to replace the one at St. Clara's Church in Chicago that burned down in 1976.

The St. Therese Shrine consists of a chapel and museum. The shrine chapel contains a stained- and faceted-glass wall depicting the traditions of Carmel. A 12-foot by 27-foot wood sculpture depicts the events in the hidden life of St. Therese — to lead many to God through her "Shower of Roses" and her "Little Way." The sculpture honors people of all races and cultures who, like Therese, go to God with confidence and love, often touching many lives in hidden but beautiful ways. At the base of the sculpture, an ornate reliquary contains the relics of St. Therese.

The St. Therese museum has not only copies of photos of the Carmelite saint but an original oil painting done by her sister Celine. On display as well are a map of North America drawn by Therese at age twelve, toys, a prayer book from her childhood, and even the chair in which she wrote her autobiography. This is said to be the best collection of relics and memorabilia outside of Therese's native France.

The property also includes a retreat house and retirement complex. Group tours can be arranged by calling the director of the shrine. The shrine is open daily 10:00 a.m.-4:00 p.m. and is closed holidays.

Schedule of Masses:

Daily: Monday-Friday: 11:30 a.m.

Devotions:

Feast of Our Lady of Mt. Carmel: July 16
Feast of St. Therese: October 1

Facilities:

Religious Bookstore
Religious Gift Shop
Museum and Retreat House

ST. MAXIMILIAN KOLBE SHRINE

1600 West Park Avenue, Libertyville, Ill. 60048
(708) 367-7800

**History
of the
Shrine:**

This particular shrine reflects the spirit of the work which St. Maximilian Kolbe began at Niepokalonow (Marytown) in Poland. St. Maximilian died in 1941 after he offered his life for a fellow prisoner in the infamous Auschwitz concentration camp. Canonized in 1982 as a "Martyr of Charity," Kolbe was called "the patron of our difficult century" by Pope John Paul II.

The life of this heroic Franciscan is captured on several mosaics depicting various moments of grace in St. Maximilian's life. The newly renovated Kolbe Shrine Chapel is situated within Marytown's exquisite eucharistic sanctuary. The church, a replica of St. Paul's-outside-the-wall in Rome, was originally built to commemorate the twenty-eighth International Eucharistic Congress held in Chicago in 1926. Perpetual Adoration of the Blessed Sacrament is maintained in this beautiful church.

The purpose of the shrine is to spread St. Maximilian's work of personal consecration to Mary Immaculate. The generic name of "Marytown" signifies the centrality of Mary in the activities and ministry at the shrine. Marytown is the National Center of the Militia Immaculate (MI) movement founded by Kolbe in 1917.

Marytown is ideal for days of recollection, group pilgrimages, and private retreats. Each summer it hosts various leadership programs of the Youth Mission for the Immaculata (YMI) for youth from the ages of eight through the late twenties. A yearlong lay volunteer program is available for young men interested in personal discernment and spiritual growth.

**Schedule
of Masses:**

Monday-Saturday: 12:00 p.m.

Devotions:

Rosary and Benediction: Daily: 7:00 p.m.
Public Adoration of the Blessed Sacrament: Daily: 6:00 a.m.-11:00 p.m.; Sunday: 9:30 a.m.
Liturgy of the Hours: Daily: 7:00 a.m., 11:45 a.m., 5:00 p.m., and 7:00 p.m.
Scripture Study: Weekly
MI Focus Group: Weekly
Secular Franciscan Fraternity: Monthly
Novenas: Weekly and Monthly

Facilities: Religious Bookstore and Gift Shop
Museum
Gathering Facilities
Overnight Accommodations

NATIONAL SHRINE OF MARY IMMACULATE QUEEN OF THE UNIVERSE

P.O. Box 832, Lombard, Ill. 60148 (708) 620-1825 or 1877

History of the Shrine:

Devotion to Our Lady as Queen originated in Ireland. An Irish nun from Donegal spoke of the title and distributed prayers and pictures of this image around the world. Shrines in honor of Mary Immaculate Queen were established, and churches, schools, and religious houses were given the title. During the same period, Cardinal Gerlier in Lyons, France gave his approval for the apostolate and inaugurated a shrine there.

To ensure the continuity and expansion of the apostolate, two centers were established for messengers, one in France and one in Galway, Ireland. During a vacation in Ireland, Ms. Barbara O'Malley and her husband Eamon learned of the devotion to Mary Immaculate Queen; they carried its message back to the United States. With the encouragement of their pastor and the approval of their bishop, the devotion to Mary Immaculate Queen was officially launched in the United States.

On May 31, 1974, the Feast of the Visitation, Mary Immaculate Queen was solemnly welcomed and enthroned in the parish of St. Pius X in Lombard, Ill. Since then countless homes, schools, and churches have enthroned her in the United States.

In May 1981, Barbara O'Malley received from the Holy Spirit a special gift of healing, which has since been confirmed by the testimonies of many who have been physically, spiritually, or emotionally healed through her ministry. A close relationship with the Mother of God is shared by Ms. O'Malley, who feels that her gift of healing was granted by Mary and reflects Mary's love for all her children. She conducts weekly healing services at St. Pius X and travels extensively around the United States and abroad, sharing her gift.

Schedule of Masses:

Sunday Vigil: 6:00 p.m.
Sunday: 7:30 a.m., 9:00 a.m., 10:30 a.m., and 12:00 p.m.
Holy Day of Obligation Vigil: 5:00 p.m.
Holy Day of Obligation: 6:30 a.m., 8:30 a.m., 10:30 a.m., and 7:00 p.m.

Devotions:

Healing Services: Sunday: 6:00 p.m.
Rosary and Benediction: Wednesday: 8:00 p.m.
Day of Prayer
Weekend Retreats

THE GROTTO OF
THE REDEMPTION

P.O. Box 376, West Bend, Iowa 50597 (515) 887-2371

**History
of the
Shrine:**

The Grotto of the Redemption at West Bend, Iowa is the largest grotto in the world. It is frequently considered "the eighth wonder of the world." The grotto represents the largest collection of minerals and petrification concentrated in any one spot in the world. Fr. Paul Dobberstein started construction on the grotto in 1912. For forty-two years, winter and summer, he labored setting ornamental rocks and gems into concrete. By his death in 1954, he had created the incredible "Grotto of the Redemption," covering one city block. Since his death, Fr. Louis Greving, who had worked with Fr. Dobberstein for eight years, has been continuing construction on the grotto.

The grotto is a composite of nine separate grottoes, each portraying a scene in the life of Christ in his work of redeeming the world. Over 100,000 people visit the grotto every year. There are systematic hourly tours through the grotto from June 1 to October 15; however, the grotto is open to visitors year-round. After every hourly tour a geological lecture is given in the rock display studio; this lecture identifies the materials used in the construction of the grotto and features an ultraviolet light display. The grotto is flooded with spotlights for evening viewing.

Adjacent to the grotto is St. Peter and Paul's Church. The Christmas chapel in the church is Fr. Dobberstein's finest work. It contains a Brazilian amethyst that weighs over three hundred pounds.

**Schedule
of Masses:**

Sunday Vigil: 5:00 p.m.
Sunday: (May 1 to September 30) 7:00 a.m., 9:00 a.m.;
(October 1 to April 30) 8:00 a.m., 10:00 a.m.

Facilities:

Restaurant (It is suggested that reservations be made when a large group is visiting the grotto.)
Free Overnight Camping with eighty electrical hookups

SHRINE OF ST. PHILIPPINE DUCHESNE

Sacred Heart Church, Mound City, Kans. 66056
(913) 795-2724

History of the Shrine:

St. Philippine Duchesne cared for the needs of the Potawatomi Indians at St. Mary's Indian Mission, twelve miles northwest of the shrine. In 1941, the late Bishop Paul C. Schulte of the Diocese of Leavenworth, Kans. (now the Archdiocese of Kansas City, Kans.) collected funds from all the parishes and people of the diocese to build a stone church and rectory complete with furnishings. The church was dedicated as a memorial shrine to St. Philippine Duchesne on September 7, 1942.

The church is 100-feet long and 40-feet wide, built of stone from St. Mary's Indian Mission. The 125-acre St. Philippine Memorial Park was purchased and developed through the efforts of Fr. Robert Pool, once pastor here, and Robert White, a Catholic layman from Overland Park, Kans. Pilgrimages have been held at both places throughout the years. The memorial park was dedicated by Archbishop Ignatius Strecker on July 3, 1988, the date of St. Philippine's Canonization by Pope John Paul II.

The Shrine of St. Philippine Duchesne will celebrate its Golden Jubilee of the Parish in 1992.

Schedule of Masses:

Sundays: 8:00 a.m.
Weekdays: 7:15 a.m.
Holy Day of Obligation: 7:00 a.m. and 7:00 p.m.
Confessions: Anytime

Devotions:

Daily: Novena Prayers to St. Philippine Duchesne
First Friday Devotions
First Saturday Devotions
Pilgrimage tours of the shrine in Mound City and the memorial park with Mass, upon request.

SHRINE OF ST. ANNE

1000 St. Anne Street, Detroit, Mich. 48216
(313) 496-1701

History of the Shrine:

St. Anne is the oldest parish in Detroit, dating back to the founding of the city in 1701. Fr. Gabriel Richard (1767-1832), the famous pastor, is buried in the church. The shrine has been approved by Rome as one of the shrines of St. Anne. The parish currently has a mostly Hispanic congregation.

A novena is celebrated from July 16-26. A former pastor, Fr. Luke Renaud, encouraged this devotion, which became an important event in Catholic life. A festival is held around the time of the novena. The Feast of Guadalupe is observed on December 12.

Schedule of Masses:

Sunday Vigil: 5:00 p.m.
Sunday: 8:30 a.m., 10:00 a.m. (Spanish), and 12:00 p.m.
Holy Day of Obligation Vigil: 5:00 p.m.
Holy Day of Obligation: 8:30 a.m., 12:00 p.m., 5:15 p.m., and 7:00 p.m. (Spanish)
Confessions: Saturday: 4:00-5:00 p.m. and 7:00-8:00 p.m.

Devotions:

Novenas: Weekly
Bible Class: Weekly (Spanish)

Facilities:

Gift Shop

Languages:

English and Spanish

THE CROSS IN THE WOODS

Indian River, Mich. 49749 (616) 238-8973

History of the Shrine:

Blessed Kateri Tekakwitha was the inspiration for this shrine in Indian River. The first pastor, Msgr. Charles D. Brophy, had a devotion to Blessed Kateri, often called the "Lily of the Mohawks." Born in 1656, the Indian maiden converted to the Catholic faith at the age of eighteen and suffered much because of her faith. Her practice of erecting crosses in the woods around the village, as reminders of her Lord and as places to pray, gave the first pastor the idea of erecting the huge cross at the Shrine.

The centerpiece of the shrine, the cross, is made from a 55-foot redwood tree. Renowned sculptor Marshall Fredericks created a bronze seven-ton image of the crucified Christ which was raised into place in 1959. The cross and the shrine have been inspiring visitors ever since.

The complex includes a large outdoor sanctuary seating 650 where the eucharist is offered during the summer months. There is also an indoor chapel for use during inclement weather.

During a visit to the shrine, a person may make the Stations of the Cross in a secluded area of the grounds and also may visit the shrine honoring Blessed Kateri, a shrine to the Blessed Mother, and a shrine honoring St. Peregrine, the patron of cancer.

Also of special interest to visitors is a collection of 525 dolls dressed in the habits of nuns who served the Church in the United States. A gift shop on the grounds offers visitors religious articles and reading material.

The peaceful quiet strength that Blessed Kateri drew from God and nature seems to permeate the shrine, beckoning people of all Christian faiths to prayer and reflection on the Lord's love for us. The shrine is staffed by Franciscans of the Sacred Heart Province of St. Louis.

The parish church is open all year. The shrine is open from April through October.

Schedule of Masses:

Last Weekend in June through Labor Day
Saturday: 4:30 p.m. and 6:00 p.m.
Sunday: 8:30 a.m. and 10:30 a.m.
Daily: 8:00 a.m. and 12:00 p.m.
Confessions: Upon request

ST. MARY'S OF MOUNT CARMEL SHRINE

260 St. Mary's Parkway, Manistee, Mich. 49660
(616) 723-3345

History of the Shrine:

St. Mary's was the first Catholic parish in Manistee and was formed in 1862. It became the mother church for the area and other parishes that followed. St. Mary's was known as the "French Church."

The present church is the third St. Mary's, constructed as a shrine in 1962. As it is located within sight of Lake Michigan, the flowing roof design and huge beams were constructed to follow the form of the sand dunes. The white marble came from Georgia, the red granite from Wisconsin, and the gray granite altar from South Dakota. The marble in the five wall murals came from Tennessee; the tile mural came from and was made in Canada. The outside Stations of the Cross came from the old church. Twenty Madonna Shrine wood carvings from Italy represent various titles of Mary.

The central focus of the shrine is a 10-foot statue of Our Lady of Mt. Carmel carved in Italy by Vincenzo Demetz, using a block of linden wood from Yugoslavia. The statue, an original, weighs 480 pounds and took over two years to complete.

The rosary is recited before daily Mass and weekend services. The months of May and October are special times to visit the shrine. The Feast of Our Lady of Mt. Carmel is on July 16 followed by a parish potluck dinner.

Schedule of Masses:

Sunday Vigil: 5:00 p.m.
Sunday: 8:30 a.m. and 11:00 a.m.
Confessions: 30 minutes before Mass

ST. MARY SHRINE

201 M-72, Mio, Mich. 48647
(517) 826-5509

History of the Shrine:

The shrine-grotto at Mio, Mich., is a mountainous structure of stone honeycombed with grottos and niches. It is actually a composite shrine of shrines in a single unit.

The name, "Our Lady of the Woods," reflects the thousands of acres of God's beautiful and majestic timberlands visible from the shrine. These were regions once home to the lumberjack but now meccas to hunters, fishermen, and tourists.

Viewed from the front, the shrine is a sloping triangle of stone. It slowly rises from the ground on two sides, ending in a peak, pointing out that all humankind's destiny is heavenwards, that the natural and temporal should be sublimated into the spiritual and eternal.

One can also visualize two arms forming from the peak of this monument as if to embrace the entire state of Michigan, the country, and the world.

The shrine-grotto is replete with symbolism, including an outdoor chapel and sanctuary. Various statues are placed throughout the grotto, including the Infant of Prague, the Resurrection, St. Hubert, and St. Anne de Beaupre. The major Marian shrines are represented by Our Lady of Lourdes, Our Lady of Fatima, Our Lady of La Salette, Our Lady of Czestochowa, the Assumption, and Our Lady of Guadalupe.

All this is dedicated to Our Lady. Everything possible has been done to make the Mother of Christ appear at home in Michigan.

Schedule of Masses:

Sunday Vigil: 5:00 p.m.
Sunday: 8:00 a.m. and 10:00 a.m.

Facilities:

Gift Shop

ASSUMPTION OF OUR LADY CHAPEL

Chapel Street, Cold Spring, Minn. 56320
(612) 685-3280

**History
of the
Shrine:**

This chapel is a memorial to the divine help received during the grasshopper plagues over a century ago. It was built through the inspiration of Bishop Peter. W. Bartholome, the fifth bishop of St. Cloud, and was solemnly dedicated on October 7, 1952, the Feast of the Most Holy Rosary.

The construction of this chapel was zealously supervised by Fr. Victor Ronellenfitsch, OSB, the pastor of St. Boniface Church, Cold Spring; the architect was his assistant, Fr. Athanase Fuchs, O.S.B. The Cold Spring Granite Company and its workers were the chief donors of the material and labor.

The 16-foot by 26-foot chapel is built of rough pink-gray granite with a reddish shingled roof topped by a belfry and a stainless-steel cross. The imported stained-glass windows depict scenes in the life of the Blessed Mother. On the wall behind the altar is a statue of the Blessed Mother.

In honor of the recent definition of the Assumption of the Blessed Mother by Pope Pius XII (1950), the chapel was given the new name of Assumption Chapel. Over the entrance of this present chapel is a tympanum with a relief of the Blessed Mother and the words: Asumpta est Maria. At her feet, two grasshoppers kneel in humble submission.

An earlier chapel, called Grasshopper Chapel, was built in 1877, commemorating the sparing of the farmers and people of Central Minnesota during the grasshopper plague through the intercession of the Blessed Virgin Mary.

In 1877, the following vow was made by the pastors and parishioners of several parishes in Central Minnesota: "To honor Mary with special devotions at the site each year. This has been done faithfully each year since 1877 on the Feast of the Assumption."

**Schedule
of Masses:**

August 15, Feast of the Assumption (Mass is celebrated by the bishop.)

NATIONAL SHRINE OF ST. ODILIA

Crosier Fathers and Brothers, Onamia, Minn. 56359-0500
(612) 532-3103

**History
of the
Shrine:**

The Shrine of St. Odilia was established in 1952 when a major relic of St. Odilia was brought to Onamia, Minn. In 1287, St. Odilia appeared to John Novelan, a lay brother of the Crosier Order in Paris, and told him she had been appointed by God to be the patron saint and the protectress of the Order of the Holy Cross. She informed him that her relics were located in an orchard in Cologne and begged him to get permission to unearth them.

St. Odilia had instructed Bro. John that her relics were to be taken to the motherhouse of the order at Huy, Belgium. Both at Cologne and on the way to Huy, various cures of physical infirmities took place.

During the French Revolution, the monastery at Huy was totally destroyed and, although the relics were saved, they were lost to the Order. In 1949, St. Odilia came back home. Her relics were returned to the Order, and a large portion of one of her bones was brought to Onamia, and now rests in her shrine here, where it is encased in a marble reliquary.

St. Odilia has promised to shower a stream of graces upon the Crosier Fathers and upon all those who invoke her aid in their hour of need. For centuries it has been the practice of the Crosier Order to bless water in honor of St. Odilia by dipping her relic in it and asking God to give it power against all diseases and bodily infirmities. Through her intercession, many are cured, especially from diseases of the eyes.

**Schedule
of Masses:** Masses are held daily.

Devotions: The St. Odilia Novena begins on the 5th and 17th of each month. The National Novena to St. Odilia is held from July 10-18. Intentions for this novena can be mailed to the shrine and visitors can participate in the novena.
St. Odilia devotional items may be obtained by writing to the shrine.

NATIONAL SHRINE OF OUR LADY OF THE MIRACULOUS MEDAL

St. Mary's Seminary, 1811 W. St. Joseph Street,
Perryville, Mo. 63775 (314) 547-8344

**History
of the
Shrine:**

The Shrine of Our Lady of the Miraculous Medal, begun in 1827 and consecrated in 1837, was officially established in 1918 by the Vincentian Fathers of the Midwest Province. The present shrine was built in 1930. The shrine is a chapel of the Church of St. Mary's of the Barrens built in 1835, one of the first churches to be consecrated west of the Mississippi. For over a century, the shrine site was the seminary for priests and brothers of the Congregation of the Mission (Vincentian Fathers).

The main religious celebration of the year is the May procession held during the first Sunday in May. The average attendance at this celebration is twenty-five hundred. Approximately ten thousand pilgrims visit the shrine annually.

**Schedule
of Masses:**

Sunday: 11:00 a.m.
Daily: 8:00 a.m.
Confessions: Monday: 7:00 p.m.

Devotions:

Novenas: Mondays: 7:15 p.m. (Miraculous Medal Novena and Mass)

Facilities:

Gift Shop: Open Monday-Friday 9:00 a.m.-12:00 p.m. and 1:00-4:00 p.m.; Saturday-Sunday 1:00-4:30 p.m. Closed holy days, holidays, and during the months of January and February.
Tours: Monday-Friday: 10:00 a.m. and 1:00 p.m.; Saturday-Sunday 1:00 p.m. and 3:00 p.m. No tours on holy days and holidays. Group tours are available by appointment only.

SHRINE OF ST. PHILIPPINE DUCHESNE

619 North Second Street, St. Charles, Mo. 63301
(314) 946-6127

History of the Shrine:

This shrine was built in honor of St. Philippine Duchesne in 1952. The sarcophagus with the remains of St. Philippine is entombed in the shrine. Philippine Duchesne was canonized a saint by Pope John Paul II on July 3, 1988.

The shrine is located on the campus of the Academy of the Sacred Heart in St. Charles, Mo. Rose Philippine Duchesne, a French Religious of the Sacred Heart, started the first free school west of the Mississippi River in a log cabin in 1818. The first permanent building was constructed in 1835.

As visitors walk through the parlors of this building, a guide tells them how Philippine Duchesne left her native France and settled in the wilderness that was St. Charles. They learn that Philippine Duchesne started other schools in Louisiana and St. Louis and how this humble beginning in the New World has blossomed into a network of nineteen Sacred Heart schools in the United States. Pilgrims may also see the room in which this saint died in 1852. The shrine is open daily for prayer and visits. A schedule of guided tours and group tour information is available.

Schedule of Masses:

There are no regularly scheduled Masses.

Devotions:

The Feast of St. Philippine Duchesne: November 18
Christmas Eve Mass
First Communion

Facilities:

Gift Shop
Museum

SHRINE OF OUR LADY OF LEVOCHA

1160 Broadway, Bedford, Ohio 44146
(216) 232-4755

**History
of the
Shrine:**   This is an outdoor shrine located on the property of the motherhouse of the Vincentian Sisters of Charity of the Diocese of Cleveland. The shrine was established in 1930. It is the only National Shrine of Our Lady of Levocha in America. The statue of Our Lady of Levocha was carved from the wood of an apple tree under the direction of Bishop John Vojtassak and was touched to the original statue of Our Lady before being shipped to the United States.

Although the early pilgrims were from Slovak backgrounds, people of all nationalities have come to honor Our Lady in individual groups or on special pilgrimage days. They come to unburden their hearts and seek consolation and aid for themselves and their loved ones.

Because there is no resident priest to offer daily Mass, pilgrims come to make private visits to Our Lady from the first Sunday of May until the official closing of the shrine on the first Sunday of October.

Devotions: Annual (traditional) Pilgrimage Day: July 2
Feasts of Ss. Joachim and Ann: July 26 (a special pilgrimage day which draws over 500 people)

Languages: Services are conducted in English and Slovak

SORROWFUL MOTHER SHRINE

4106 Street, Route #269, Bellevue, Ohio 44811
(419) 483-3435

**History
of the
Shrine:**

The shrine was founded in 1847 on four acres. It now encompasses 140 acres, of which seventy are virgin forest, accommodating the Stations of the Cross, six grottoes, various statues, and over a mile of paved paths. The Stations were added during World War I, the Lourdes and Sepulchre grottoes in the 1930s, and finally the grottoes to Our Lady of Guadalupe and Assumption.

The cafeteria and religious goods store were added in 1960 as was the outdoor pavilion, which seats one thousand.

On Sundays and holy days, devout processions are led by the clergy, making stops at each sacred grotto along the Way of the Cross. Frequent candlelight processions, outdoor Masses, and the old shrine chapel provide devotional experiences that keep pilgrims returning again and again.

The ethnic celebrations are a big attraction but many pilgrims come seeking solace in the peaceful wooded area.

**Schedule
of Masses:**

Sunday Vigil: 4:30 p.m.
Sunday: 9:00 a.m. and 11:00 a.m.
Daily: 11:00 a.m. and 7:00 p.m. (May-October)
Holy Day of Obligation Vigil: 4:30 p.m.
Holy Day of Obligation: 9:00 a.m. and 11:00 a.m.
Confessions: Daily: 10:30 a.m.; Sunday: 8:00 a.m., 9:00 a.m., and 10:00 a.m.

Devotions:

Processions, Rosary, Benediction: Weekly (Sunday)
Novenas: Monthly
Days of Recollection: Weekly

Facilities:

Religious Bookstore
Gift Shop
Cafeteria

Languages:

English, Italian, Caldean, Slovak, Spanish, Slovenian, Hungarian, and Polish

SHRINE OF THE WEEPING MADONNA OF MARIAPOCH

17486 Mumford Road, Burton, Ohio 44021
(216) 834-8807 or (216) 834-4078

History of the Shrine:

The Shrine of the Weeping Madonna of Mariapoch in Burton, Ohio, originates from the shrine in Mariapoch, Hungary. The shrine in Hungary was established in 1696 when an icon — a Greek painting of Our Lady, somewhat like that of our own Perpetual Help — was seen to shed tears. From each eye of the picture, tears coursed down Our Lady's face, drop by drop. For eighteen days this phenomenon continued until December 8. There were many miracles. Crowds came to Poch from all the neighboring villages to see and pray before the Weeping Madonna. An investigation by ecclesial authorities could not find a natural explanation for the tears.

The Shrine of the Weeping Madonna in Mariapoch was held in high and pious esteem by the people of Hungary. The Hungarian immigrants carried the memory and experience of the shrine to distant lands, including the United States. To give honor to the Weeping Madonna, an anonymous person donated fifty acres of wooded land in Welshfield, Ohio. The first chapel and the shrine erected to honor the Weeping Madonna, was dedicated and blessed in 1956 by the Most Rev. Nicholas T. Elko. Outdoor Stations of the Cross provide atmosphere and meditation. All visitors are welcome, Tuesdays through Sundays.

Schedule of Masses:

Sunday: 8:30 a.m. (oratory) and 4:00 p.m. (outdoor shrine altar)
Holy Day of Obligation Vigil: 6:00 p.m. (oratory)
Holy Day of Obligation: 9:00 a.m. (oratory)
Confessions: Sunday: 3:00-3:45 p.m.

Devotions:

Marian Devotions: Sunday, following the 4:00 p.m. liturgy
Days of Recollection, One-Day Retreats
Public anointing of the sick: First Sunday of the month (May-October)

Facilities:

Gift Shop
Bookstore
Cafeteria
Mosaic and Byzantine Art Studio
Crucifixion Pavilion

Languages:

English, Ruthenian, and Hungarian

BASILICA AND SHRINE OF OUR LADY OF CONSOLATION

315 Clay Street, Carey, Ohio 43316 (419) 396-7107 or (419) 396-3355

History of the Shrine:

Since 1875, countless numbers of pilgrims have journeyed to the Basilica and Shrine of Our Lady of Consolation to express their devotion to Mary, Consoler of the Afflicted. Devotion to this image of Mary was first expressed by St. Ignatius of Antioch in the second century. In the seventeenth century when an outbreak of bubonic plague devastated the population, the people of the Grand Duchy of Luxembourg began praying to Mary, and a small chapel was built on the outskirts of town to enshrine her image. In 1652, Pope Innocent X established a confraternity at the little shrine.

The devotion flourished for two hundred years then spread to North America, where the first shrine was established by Fr. Joseph P. Gloden at the mission of Carey, Ohio. The people of Carey constructed and dedicated a new frame church to house the image. A replica of the original image was brought to nearby Frenchtown, and from there a solemn procession took it to the little church at Carey.

On April 28, 1878, Pope Leo XIII established a confraternity at Carey, thus firmly establishing the devotion of Our Lady of Consolation in this country. In 1925, a new and larger church was dedicated, and in 1971 Pope Paul VI designated it a minor basilica.

The shrine is a noted location for the healing of body, mind, and spirit through the intercession of Our Lady of Consolation.

The shrine is open for prayer twenty-four hours a day. Pilgrimage groups visit the shrine from May through October; during the month of August, groups of many nationalities join in the festivities. People of various nationalities come year-round by car, and six different Catholic rites are celebrated here May through October.

Schedule of Masses:

Sunday Vigil: 5:30 p.m.
Sunday: 8:00 a.m., 10:00 a.m., and 12:00 p.m.
Daily: 7:00 a.m. and 11:00 a.m.
Saturday: 7:00 a.m. and 11:00 a.m.

Devotions:

Benediction of the Blessed Sacrament, healing service: Sunday: 2:30 p.m. (including Marian devotions)
Rosary Procession: Every Sunday from May to October with statues

carried in procession
Candlelight Procession and Mass: August 14

Facilities: Renewal Center (for retreats)
Overnight Accommodations
Cafeteria
Gift Shop
Thirty-five acre outdoor shrine park: ample car and bus parking

NATIONAL FRIARY AND SHRINE OF ST. ANTHONY

Franciscan Friars, 5000 Colerain Avenue, Cincinnati, Ohio 45223 (513) 541-2146

History of the Shrine:

A devout member of St. Francis Seraph parish, Mr. A. Joseph Nurre, and his wife bought a country estate high above Cincinnati for the local Franciscan Friars and promised to build a monastery, a home for infirm friars, and a chapel to serve as a Franciscan novitiate. The cornerstone was laid and blessed by Fr. Jerome, a former provincial superior, in 1888. In October, the first friars moved into the original estate house and on Thanksgiving Day, 1889, Archbishop Henry Elder of Cincinnati consecrated the chapel. The first investitures at Mt. Airy, the familiar name for the friary and shrine, took place on the Feast of the Assumption in 1890.

The chapel was dedicated to St. Anthony; however, it was never intended to be a shrine. Gradually, though, people began to make private pilgrimages to the chapel and, as the number of visitors increased, the chapel became known as St. Anthony's Shrine. Furnishings for the shrine came from France, Belgium, Bavaria, Holland, and Austria. Originally the shrine contained eight side altars. Above the high altar were two large paintings portraying scenes from the life of St. Anthony; however, these paintings were covered over when the shrine was redecorated in 1978.

In January 1928, a small group of friends met at the friary at the invitation of Fr. Stephen Hoffmann, OFM, in order to establish a society to further devotion to St. Anthony and to the upkeep of the shrine. They built a beautiful shelterhouse in which to serve refreshments to visitors, which has now been replaced by the present hall. The society is also responsible for welcoming and accommodating visitors and for organizing the annual festival in September.

Schedule of Masses:

Sunday: 10:00 a.m. (shrine)
Weekdays: 7:30 a.m. (shrine)
Saturday: 8:15 a.m. (shrine)
Holy Day of Obligation: 10:00 a.m. (shrine)
Novena Mass: Tuesday: 6:00 p.m. (chapel)
Confessions: Upon request

Devotions:

Novena to St. Anthony: Tuesday: 2:30-7:30 p.m. (chapel) (lasting one-half hour)
Feast of St. Anthony: June 13 (Novenas are held on the nine Sundays before.)

ST. PAUL SHRINE

*(Conversion of St. Paul Church) East 40th Street and Euclid Avenue, Cleveland, Ohio 44103
(216) 431-8854*

**History
of the
Shrine:** Established in 1931 as the Church of the Conversion of St. Paul and Shrine of the Blessed Sacrament, the church came to be known simply as St. Paul Shrine. The Monastery of the Poor Clares of Perpetual Adoration is attached to the shrine. Nuns maintain prayerful vigil before the Blessed Sacrament exposed throughout the day. Capuchin Franciscans presently minister to the sisters, the small parish community, and visitors.

**Schedule
of Masses:** Sunday: 11:30 a.m.
Daily: 12:00 p.m.
Holy Day of Obligation: 7:00 a.m. and 12:00 p.m.
Confessions: Monday-Saturday: 11:30 a.m.

Devotions: Novenas: Weekly
Rosary: Weekly
Perpetual Adoration of the Blessed Sacrament: Daily

Facilities: Daily meal for the needy

NATIONAL AMERICAN SHRINE OF OUR LADY OF LOURDES

21281 Chardon Road, Euclid, Ohio 44117 (216) 481-8232

History of the Shrine:

The shrine and grotto of Our Lady of Lourdes at Euclid, Ohio, is a copy of the original shrine in Lourdes, France. In 1922, while visiting the world famous shrine at Lourdes, Mother Mary of St. John Berchman McGarvey was inspired to erect a similar grotto on the property of the Good Shepherd Sisters in Euclid. Fr. Pere Ekert, a Dominican priest, gave the sisters a piece of stone hewn of the rock on which the Blessed Mother stood when she appeared to Bernadette. Two pieces of the stone are now imbedded in the grotto, and the other is located in a reliquary in the Gift Shop.

The Most Rev. Bishop Schrembs, D.D., blessed and dedicated the grotto on Trinity Sunday, May 30, 1926. On the occasion of a city-wide pilgrimage, October 7, 1928, Archbishop Schrembs conferred the title of National American Shrine of Our Lady of Lourdes.

Since the erection of the shrine, pilgrims have come to honor Our Lady and to place before her their petitions. Hundreds of favors, spiritual and temporal, have been granted. Today, the Trinitarian Sisters operate the shrine where their novitiate is also located, as is their provincial house in the United States.

Schedule of Masses:

Sunday: 8:00 a.m. (chapel) and 9:30 a.m. (grotto)
Daily: Monday, Wednesday-Friday: 7:00 a.m.
Tuesday: 5:00 p.m.
Saturday: 8:00 a.m.
Holy Day of Obligation: 8:00 a.m.
Holiday: 8:00 a.m.
Confessions: During Novenas only

Devotions:

Stations of the Cross: Sunday: 3:00 p.m. with
Rosary Procession, Homily and Benediction: 4:00 p.m.
Our Lady of Lourdes Novenas: February 3-11
Triduum and Feast of St. Ann: July 24-26
Assumption Novena: August 7-15
Candlelight Procession, Rosary, and Mass
First Sunday of October: Fall Festival, Bazaar

Facilities:

Gift Shop
Cafeteria

SHRINE OF THE HOLY RELICS

P.O. Box 117, 2291 St. Johns Road, Maria Stein, Ohio 45860
(419) 925-4532

**History
of the
Shrine:**

The Shrine of the Holy Relics contains a rare collection of holy relics brought from Italy and donated to the Sisters of the Precious Blood in 1875 by a priest from Milwaukee. In 1892, a beautiful new chapel was opened to house the relics. During this time relics were added to the collection by the Rev. Francis de Sales Brunner, the first Precious Blood priest to come to America. Other relics have been donated, including those of Archbishop McNicholas and Archbishop Alter, both of Cincinnati.

The relics are the remembrances of the saints of God. The remains of the martyrs were venerated in the catacombs of Rome. In the Middle Ages, pilgrimages were made to shrines that housed these sacred remains for the purpose of prayer. At Maria Stein, the sacred tradition of the Church is continued as people come from near and far in the spirit of prayer and hope to honor the memory of those holy men and women of God. The large number of people who visit the shrine indicates the many graces and favors granted by God through the intercession of his saints.

The shrine is staffed by the Sisters of the Precious Blood. Since there is no resident chaplain, inquiries regarding Masses should be made.

Devotions: Retreats: Scheduled throughout the year

Facilities: Religious Bookstore
Retreat House
Overnight Accommodations
Gift Shop
Cafeteria

NATIONAL SHRINE OF OUR LADY OF LEBANON

2759 North Lipkey Road, North Jackson, Ohio 44451
(216) 538-3351

History of the Shrine:

The National Shrine of Our Lady of Lebanon is an exact replica of the original shrine in Harissa, Lebanon. This shrine is Maronite Rite Catholic and was established in 1963 to bring together all Lebanese, Syrians, and Americans through the intercession of Our Lady of Lebanon. The shrine project received the approval of Pope John XXIII and Most Rev. Emmet M. Walsh, bishop of Youngstown.

The main religious celebration of the year is the Feast of the Assumption in August. The three-day festivities attract numerous pilgrims. The Holy Week and Easter celebrations traditional to Maronite Catholics provide a spiritual and cultural experience.

Schedule of Masses:

Sunday Vigil: 7:00 p.m.
Sunday: 10:00 a.m. and 7:00 p.m.
Daily: Monday-Thursday: 5:30 p.m.
Friday: 12:00 p.m.
Confessions: Half-hour before each weekend liturgy, or by appointment

Devotions:

Rosary: Daily before Mass
Vespers to Our Lady of Lebanon: Wednesday: after 5:30 p.m. Mass
First Friday Liturgy in honor of the Sacred Heart of Jesus: 11:00 a.m.
Holy Hour, followed by 12:00 p.m. Mass
First Saturday Liturgy in honor of the Immaculate Heart of Mary: 8:00 a.m.
Feast of Our Lady of Lebanon: First Sunday in May
Annual Assumption Pilgrimage: August 13-15

Nine-Day Novenas: March: St. Joseph
June: St. Anthony
September: St. Theresa
October: St. Jude
December: Infant Jesus of Prague

Facilities:

Religious Bookstore
Gift Shop

Languages:

English, Aramaic, and Lebanese

SHRINE OF OUR LADY COMFORTER OF THE AFFLICTED

517 S. Belle Vista Avenue, Youngstown, Ohio 44509
(216) 799-1888

History of the Shrine:

The Shrine of Our Lady, Comforter of the Afflicted was established in Youngstown, Ohio, by Hungarian Franciscans who fled their homeland shortly after World War II. The shrine in Youngstown is a replica of the original shrine in Transylvania, Hungary, which was closed by the Communist regime.

The shrine in Youngstown continues the charism and the spirit of Our Lady, Comforter of the Afflicted in Transylvania and serves people across the country, especially those of Hungarian origin. The shrine is staffed by the Franciscan Order.

Schedule of Masses:

Sunday: 8:00 a.m., 9:00 a.m., and 12:00 p.m.
Holy Day of Obligation: 8:00 a.m., 9:00 a.m., 12:00 p.m., and 7:30 p.m.
Confessions: Thursday: 6:30-7:00 p.m.; Saturday: 7:00-8:00 p.m.

Devotions:

Novenas: Weekly and annually
Rosary: Weekly
Retreats: For groups, upon request
Holy Hour of Eucharistic Adoration: Weekly
Pilgrimage on Pentecost Sunday: Annually

Facilities:

Religious Bookstore
Cafeteria
Counseling Center
Gift Shop
Cultural Center

Languages:

English, Hungarian, and German

SHRINE OF
THE NATIVITY

Pilgrim Road, Bethlehem, S.Dak. 57708 (605) 787-4606

**History
of the
Shrine:**

The shrine was established by the Benedictine Fathers on property donated by Mr. Louis Storm in 1952. Under the direction of the Rev. Gilbert Stack, a monk from Conception Abbey, and assistance from volunteers from various countries, the Bethlehem Cave and the Shrine of the Nativity were further developed.

All year round, but especially during the Christmas season, people from different denominations and parts of the country seek a peaceful haven in this grotto. In a busy, modern world, it is so easy to forget the Way, the Truth, and the Light that came from a cave in Bethlehem two thousand years ago.

**Schedule
of Masses:**

Sunday: 12:00 p.m.
Holy Day of Obligation: 12:00 p.m.
Daily: 12:00 p.m.
Confessions: Upon request

Devotions:

Retreats: By reservation only
Devotions and Bible Reading: Daily

Facilities:

Gift Shop
Retreat Facility for Youth
Office for Religious Pilgrimages
Printing Facilities

THE HOUSE OF MARY SHRINE, HOLY INNOCENTS MEMORIAL

Lewis and Clark Lake, Yankton, S.Dak. 57078
(605) 239-4532

History of the Shrine:

The House of Mary Shrine was started in 1971 by a group of interested lay people in order to honor Mary, the Mother of God. It has always had the approval and blessing of the bishop.

The shrine is located on fifty acres of land on the Lewis and Clark Lake by Yankton, S.Dak. The lake attracts people from all over the country and the world.

The shrine has a Chapel of St. Joseph where Masses are celebrated. A statue of Mary is on the hillside by the Rosary of Roses. Stations of the Cross wind up the hill to the three large Crosses on the top of the hill. A quiet place for contemplative prayer is the meditation area, which includes statues of St. Michael the Archangel and Moses and the Ten Commandments.

The grounds also contain small shrines to popular saints such as St. Teresa, St. Francis of Assisi, St. Benedictine, St. Isidore, along with a small memorial shrine to the Holy Innocents. Four hermitages in the wooded area are open for retreats and quiet praying.

The Sacred Heart Pond, blessed and dedicated by the bishop to the Sacred Heart of Jesus and Immaculate Heart of Mary, has a rosary made from stones around it. This rosary is prayed frequently by pilgrims.

Schedule of Masses:

Sunday: 1:00-5:00 p.m. (Adoration of the Blessed Sacrament, Chapel of St. Joseph)
First Saturday: 9:00 a.m. (Mass of the Blessed Virgin Mary, Chapel of St. Joseph)

Devotions:

Rosary: Saturday: 8:00 a.m. (Chapel of St. Joseph)
Sunday: Medjugorje Prayer Group 3:00-4:00 p.m., Rosary: 4:00 p.m.
Easter Sunday Sunrise Service (all faiths welcome) Prayers, hymns, and Scripture read.
First Sunday in May: May Crowning of Mary
First Sunday in October: Rosary Rally (candlelight)
December 28: Holy Innocents (Prayer for the reparation of murders of abortion, Chapel of St. Joseph)
Pilgrimages come frequently. They often bring a priest, and a Mass is said in the Chapel of St. Joseph (reservations required). The shrine is open year-round.

DICKEYVILLE GROTTO

Box 427, West Main Street,
Dickeyville, Wis. 53808
(608) 568-7519

History of the Shrine:

The grotto was built by Fr. Mathias Wernerus from 1925-29. The dedication took place on September 14, 1930. The grotto is made up of several shrines, gardens, and fences. Made of stone, mortar, and brightly colored objects from around the world, it is dedicated to the unity of two great American ideals — love of God and love of country.

The grotto was the own creation of Fr. Mathias who used pieces of glass, gems, pottery, shells, fossils, corals, quartz, agates, and ores, among other materials, to piece his design together.

The inside of the grotto contains a statue of Our Lady and the Infant Jesus. On the outside walls are represented the Seven Gifts and the Twelve Fruits of the Holy Ghost. The little shrine serves as a repository altar for the Corpus Christi Procession.

Approximately fifteen thousand to twenty thousand people visit the grotto annually.

Schedule of Masses:

Sunday Vigil: 4:00 p.m. and 8:00 p.m.
Sunday: 8:00 a.m. and 10:00 a.m.
Holy Day of Obligation Vigil: 4:00 p.m. and 8:00 p.m.
Holy Day of Obligation: 8:00 a.m. and 10:00 a.m.
Confessions: Half-hour before Masses

Devotions:

Novenas: Weekly
Rosary: Daily
Bible Class: Weekly

Facilities:

Religious Bookstore
Gift Shop (May-October)
Guided Tours: Daily (June-August); Weekends (May, September, October)

HOLY HILL – MARY HELP OF CHRISTIANS

1525 Carmel Road, Hubertus, Wis. 53033 (414) 628-1838

History of the Shrine:

The stories of the Indians tell that a cross was erected by Marquette himself on the peak of what is now known as Holy Hill. The Irish heard of the story from the Catholic Indians and, in 1855, Fr. Francis Paulhuber, pastor of an Irish parish in Goldendale, Wis., purchased the property. Three years later, he raised and blessed a 15-foot, wooden cross there.

Because of the growing number of people making pilgrimages to Holy Hill, a small chapel was constructed and dedicated to Mary Help of Christians in 1863. This chapel housed the shrine statue, which was purchased in 1876 and brought to Holy Hill two years later. The day the statue arrived, it was carried in procession by eighteen young girls, escorted by horsemen and pilgrims, from St. Huberts in Hubertus, Wis., a small town eight miles east of Holy Hill.

The popularity of Holy Hill as a place of pilgrimage continued to grow, and it soon became necessary to build a larger chapel. This chapel was dedicated by Archbishop Heiss of Milwaukee in 1881. In 1906, the Discalced Carmelites of Bavaria were invited by Archbishop Messmer to staff the shrine. The Carmelites accepted the invitation and sent several of their order to establish a monastery at the shrine. A new church of Romanesque design was dedicated in 1931, and an adjoining monastery was added seven years later.

Schedule of Masses:

Sunday Vigil: 4:30 p.m.
Sunday: 8:00 a.m., 9:30 a.m. (summer), 10:00 a.m. (winter), 11:00 a.m., 12:00 p.m. (summer), and 12:30 p.m. (winter)
Daily: Monday-Friday: 6:00 a.m. and 11:00 a.m.
Holy Day of Obligation: 6:00 a.m. and 11:00 a.m.
Confessions: 30 minutes before each weekend Mass; 15 minutes before the 11:00 a.m. daily Mass; and upon request

Devotions:

Novenas: Monthly
Marian Devotions: Weekly
Rosary: Weekly (May-October)
Stations of the Cross: Weekly (during Lent)
Sacred Concerts: Seasonally
Group Pilgrimages: Upon request

Facilities: Religious Bookstore/Gift Shop
Old Monastery Inn (Cafeteria)
Overnight Accommodations

SHRINE OF OUR LADY OF GOOD HELP

4047 Chapel Drive, New Franken, Wis. 54129
(414) 866-2571

**History
of the
Shrine:**   The shrine is devoutly called by many "The Chapel." The first log chapel was built in 1858 to enclose the spot where Mary allegedly appeared to Adele Brice. This chapel was replaced by a larger structure in 1861, which served until 1880. Ever increasing devotion to the Mother of God was heightened by the miraculous preservation of the chapel and its grounds from the encircling, devastating Peshtigo fire. Hence, a larger chapel was built in 1880. When this chapel was razed in 1941, to permit the erection of the present chapel, the two stumps of trees where Mary had appeared were found beneath the floor of the crypt. A statue of Mary with hands extended now occupies this spot. Bishop Paul Rhode dedicated the present chapel in 1942.

The ground floor of the chapel provides accommodations for the celebration of Mass and private devotions. The spacious sanctuary graced with a large statute of Mary enables the devout to circle in a rosary pilgrimage. The crypt below is greatly venerated as the statue of Mary recalls the scene of the alleged apparitions of 1858.

The chapel is open daily.

**Schedule
of Masses:**   Tuesday: 8:00 a.m.
Last Sunday in May: 10:00 a.m.
August 15: 6:00 a.m., 7:00 a.m., 8:00 a.m., 9:00 a.m., and 10:00 a.m.

Devotions: Rosary Novena: Tuesday: 9:00 a.m.
Holy Hour: Sunday: 2:00 p.m.

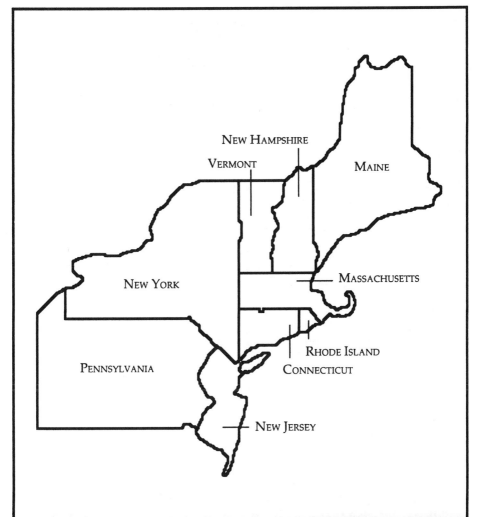

NEW HAMPSHIRE

VERMONT

MAINE

NEW YORK

MASSACHUSETTS

PENNSYLVANIA

RHODE ISLAND

CONNECTICUT

NEW JERSEY

NORTHEAST

LOURDES IN LITCHFIELD

Route 118 (East Street), P.O. Box 667, Litchfield, Conn. 06759 (203) 567-8434

History of the Shrine:

The shrine was founded as a gift to Mary for the first Marian year. It is a fairly precise replica of the original shrine in Lourdes, France; even the terrain is similar. The devotions and hymns are essentially faithful to the Lourdes tradition, but all Marian devotions are encouraged.

The Montfort Missionaries serve the shrine. The Blessing of Motorcycles and Polish Day are the two most celebrated events of the year. Approximately 35,000 people visit the shrine annually.

Schedule of Masses:

Sunday: 11:30 a.m.
Masses are also held on Marian feasts and pilgrimage days.
Confessions: Sunday: 2:15-3:15 p.m.

Devotions:

Stations of the Cross: All days of pilgrimage
Triduum: Annually
Assumption and anointing of sick: Annually
Rosary: Weekly (also on feast days and pilgrimage days)
Youth Day: Biannually
Blessing of Motorcycles: Annually
Retreats: Occasionally
Prayer for Healing: Annually
Celebrate Love (for engaged/married couples): Annually

Facilities:

Retreat Center
Gift Shop
Cafeteria

Languages:

English, French, Italian, and Spanish

LA SALETTE SHRINE

947 Park Street (Route 118), Attleboro, Mass. 02703
(617) 222-5410

History of the Shrine: The shrine was officially opened on December 8, 1953 (a Marian Year) with the First Christmas Festival of Lights. Since then, the grounds have been expanded and additional buildings constructed. It was founded and has always been staffed by the Missionaries of Our Lady of La Salette. The focus of the shrine ministries is reconciliation — the charism of the La Salette Missionaries.

The important celebrations of the year include: The Feast of Our Lady of La Salette; Ethnic Pilgrimage Days for Poles, Franco-Americans, Portuguese, and Vietnamese; and the Christmas Festival of Lights.

Schedule of Masses: Sunday Vigil: 6:30 p.m.
Sunday: 12:10 p.m.
Daily: 12:10 p.m.; Monday-Saturday: 6:30 p.m.
Schedule of Confessions: Monday-Friday: 1:00-2:00 p.m.;
Saturday-Sunday: 1:00-5:00 p.m.
Holy Day of Obligation Vigil: 6:30 p.m.
Holy Day of Obligation: 12:10 p.m.

Devotions: Novenas: Tuesdays 12:10 p.m. and 6:30 p.m..

Rosary: Weekdays 11:45 p.m. and 6:00 p.m.
Bible Class: September-May
Retreats: Year-round

Facilities: Religious Bookstore
Counseling Center
Gift Shop
Cafeteria
Retreat House

Languages: English, French, and Spanish

ST. CLEMENT'S
EUCHARISTIC SHRINE

1105 Boylston Street, Boston, Mass. 02215 (617) 266-5999

History of the Shrine:

St. Clement's Eucharistic Shrine was established on May 3, 1945, by the late Richard Cardinal Cushing, as the official archdiocesan shrine for eucharistic adoration. The shrine is intended to be a center for worship and growth in the mystery of the eucharist; it provides a prayerful atmosphere for the celebration of the eucharistic sacrifice and all-day exposition of the Blessed Sacrament.

The facilities of the shrine and adjacent seminary are also available for priests who wish to spend some time away from their administrative duties to rest a while with the Lord.

A Christmas party and play are presented by the seminarians. The Easter Triduum is also celebrated.

Schedule of Masses:

Saturday: 11:00 a.m.
Sunday: 11:00 a.m.
Weekday: 6:45 a.m., 12:10 p.m., and 4:00 p.m.
Confessions: Saturday: 10:00-10:45 a.m. and 5:00-6:00 p.m.; Sunday: 10:00-10:45 a.m.; and upon request
Holy Day of Obligation: Regular schedule

Devotions:

Rosary: Daily, except Sundays (followed by Evening Prayer and Benediction)
Exposition of the Blessed Sacrament: Monday-Friday: 7:00 a.m.-7:00 p.m.; Saturday-Sunday: 11:00 a.m.-7:00 p.m.

Facilities:

Library
Our Lady of Grace Seminary

Languages:

English, Italian, and Spanish

MADONNA, QUEEN OF THE UNIVERSE NATIONAL SHRINE

111 Orient Avenue, East Boston, Mass. 02128 (617) 569-2100

History of the Shrine:

The National Shrine of Madonna, Queen of the Universe was founded in 1954. A 35-foot statue of the Madonna was created by renowned Italian sculptor Arrigo Minerbi, who designed his statue according to the noble face of Our Blessed Lord imprinted upon the Holy Shroud of Turin. The statue is an exact copy of one which stands on top of Monte Mario in Rome. Cardinal Cushing approved the plans for construction of the shrine, and it was he who celebrated the first Holy Mass there in 1960. The main church was dedicated in November 1987. The shrine is operated by the Don Orione Fathers.

Pope John XXIII once called shrines "clinics for souls." It is hoped that this shrine will also be a clinic for many souls. This thought continues to inspire and animate the friends of the shrine and is the reason why so many pilgrims have returned again and again. The shrine has a special relationship with the Order Sons of Italy in America who has aided it in past endeavors.

Schedule of Masses:

Weekdays: 8:30 a.m. and 7:30 p.m.
Sunday Vigil: 7:30 p.m.
Sunday: 11:00 a.m. and 4:30 p.m.
Holy Day of Obligation Vigil: 7:30 p.m.
Holy Day of Obligation: 8:30 a.m. and 7:30 p.m.
Confessions: Saturday: 6:30-7:30 p.m.; also upon request

Devotions:

Rosary: Weekdays: 7:00 p.m.; Sundays and Holy Days of Obligation: 3:30 p.m.
Adoration of the Blessed Sacrament: Sundays and Holy Days of Obligation: 3:45 p.m.
Madonna Queen of the Universe: Sunday after Assumption
Dedication of the Shrine: November 2
Blessed Louis Orione: March 12

Novenas
Madonna Queen of the Universe: August
Immaculate Conception: November 29-Dec. 7
Christmas: December 16-24
Blessed Louis Orione: March 3-12
First Saturday Devotions

Month of May: Devotions before 7:30 p.m. Mass
May Procession: Last Sunday in May

Facilities: Gift Shop
Cultural Center
Pilgrim Function Hall

Languages: English, Spanish, Italian, and Latin

OUR LADY OF FATIMA SHRINE

101 Summer Street, Holliston, Mass. 01746 (617) 429-2144

History of the Shrine: Our Lady of Fatima Shrine at Holliston, Mass., built and directed by the Xaverian Missionaries, is one of the leading centers of Marian devotion in New England. The purpose of the shrine is to make known the message of Our Lady of Fatima, a truly missionary message, and to offer a tranquil setting near the mission center where people can come to pray and meditate.

Fatima Shrine was established by Fr. Henry Frassineti, a Xaverian priest who came to the United States after spending eighteen years as a missionary in China where he built what is believed to be the first chapel in the world dedicated to Our Lady of Fatima.

The first Xaverian house was an abandoned farmhouse. The unkempt, swampy grounds were gradually transformed into a pleasant garden with hills, ponds, and winding paths. The Hill of Fatima, with the altar for the celebration of Mass, was the original shrine. Over the years it has been joined with many other public worship places such as Fatima, Stations of the Cross, *The Pieta,* Calvary, Rosary Walk, etc. The shrine is an inspiration to all visitors who seek a deeper spiritual life closer to Jesus through Mary, the Mother of God.

Schedule of Masses: Sunday: 11:00 a.m.
Confessions: 3:00-5:00 p.m.; also upon request

Devotions: World Mission Rosary: Sunday: 3:00 p.m.
Bible Class: Fridays
Retreats: Weekly
Public Worship of the Blessed Sacrament: Sunday: 3:30 p.m.

Facilities: Religious Bookstore
Gift Shop
Counseling Center
Cultural Center
World Mission Rosary Makers

Languages: French, Italian, English, Spanish, Portuguese, and Japanese

ST. JOSEPH THE WORKER SHRINE

37 Lee Street, Box 1276, Lowell, Mass. 01853 (508) 458-6346

**History
of the
Shrine:**

From a modest settlement of Indians and English settlers grouped at the junction of the Concord and Merrimack Rivers evolved in the nineteenth century the largest concentration of cotton and weaving mills in the hemisphere.

By 1836, the year of its incorporation, Lowell saw eight new mills go into operation. In 1864, several manufacturers had commissioned Samuel P. Marin to visit his native Quebec Province to recruit labor for Lowell's mills. The Canadian response was overwhelming. As their numbers increased, these Franco-Americans would now become concerned of their spiritual heritage and religious situation.

From 1866 to 1868, the Franco-American population of the Archdiocese of Boston had already doubled. Most. Rev. John J. Williams desperately needed a French-speaking priest who could take up residence in Lowell for the spiritual needs of these Franco-Canadian immigrants now arriving in Lawrence, Lowell, Haverhill, Marlboro, and the Merrimack Valley.

In 1867, Archbishop Williams went to Burlington, Vt.; there he met a provincial of the Oblates of Mary Immaculate from Montreal, Canada. He made a most urgent plea for missionaries who could come to Lowell to form a French-speaking parish. The following year, two Oblate missionaries arrived in Lowell from Montreal.

Fr. Lucien Lagler and Fr. Andre M. Garin, OMI, immediately began preaching a parish mission for the French-speaking population in the basement of St. Patrick's Church. The response was so overwhelming that Fr. Garin decided to purchase a church building from a society of spiritualists. The first Mass at the new site, held shortly afterward, was on the Feast of St. Joseph; Fr. Garin chose the saint as the patron for the parish.

St. Joseph's Church became the religious and social center of the Franco-American population. The lower level of the church would serve as halls for all sodalities and societies meetings, Recent immigrants from Canada would look for work and would meet on the church steps after the liturgy for interviews with bosses and employers of the Lowell mills.

The church was rededicated as the Shrine of St. Joseph, Patron of Workers, on May 10, 1956, by Archbishop Richard J. Cushing of

Boston and Bishop Jean Louis Collignon, OMI, of the Diocese of Les Cayes, Haiti.

The shrine is open daily 7:00 a.m.-6:00 p.m. and currently serves the sacramental needs of the Greater Lowell Metropolitan Area.

Schedule of Masses: Sunday Vigil: 4:00 p.m., 5:00 p.m., and 6:00 p.m.
Sunday: 8:15 a.m., 10:15 a.m., and 11:30 a.m.
Daily: Monday-Friday: 8:00 a.m., 12:00 p.m., and 5:40 p.m.
Holy Day of Obligation Vigil: 4:00 p.m. and 5:30 p.m.
Holy Day of Obligation: 8:00 a.m., 11:00 a.m., 12:00 p.m., 4:00 p.m., and 5:30 p.m.
Saturday: 8:00 a.m., 12:00 p.m., 4:00 p.m., and 5:30 p.m.
Confessions: Monday-Friday: 10:00 a.m.-12:55 p.m. and 4:30-5:25 p.m.; Saturday: 10:00 a.m.-12:55 p.m.

Devotions: Rosary: Monday-Friday: Joyful Mysteries: 7:30 a.m.; Sorrowful Mysteries: 11:40 a.m.; Glorious Mysteries: 5:10 p.m.
Morning Prayer: Monday-Friday: 7:55 a.m.
Exposition of the Blessed Sacrament: Monday-Saturday: 8:30 a.m.
Evening Prayer: Monday-Friday: 5:30 p.m.
Novenas: Wednesday (after all Masses): St. Joseph and Blessed Eugene de Mazenod

BASILICA AND SHRINE OF OUR LADY OF PERPETUAL HELP

1545 Tremont Street, Roxbury, Mass. 02120 (617) 445-2600

History of the Shrine:

In 1854, Pope Pius IX commissioned the Redemptorists to spread devotion to Our Lady of Perpetual Help and gave the original picture to their care; it is cherished in their church on Via Merulana in Rome. When the Basilica of Our Lady of Perpetual Help was constructed in 1871, a magnificent altar of Carrara marble, in honor of Our Lady of Perpetual Help, was built as its centerpiece. The church was named a basilica in 1954 by Pope Pius XII.

The shrine the church contains a beautiful picture of Our Mother of Perpetual Help where many visitors have come to plead for favors. There is proof of these favors being answered. Beneath the picture are two vases containing crutches, canes, and casts. The first miracle recorded at the shrine occurred on August 18, 1883, when a little crippled girl who was making a novena suddenly gave her crutches to her brother, thanked the Lord, and walked out of the church. More cures followed, and newspapers across the country hailed the mission church shrine as Lourdes in the Land of the Puritans.

Today, more than one hundred years later, devotions in honor of the Mother of Perpetual Help are held at the shrine every Wednesday of the year. The main celebrations of the year include Easter, the Feast of Our Lady of Perpetual Help, and the Feasts of St. Alphonsus and St. John Neumann. The shrine is staffed by the Redemptorists and the School Sisters of Notre Dame.

Schedule of Masses:

Sunday Vigil: 4:00 p.m.
Sunday: 8:00 a.m., 10:00 a.m., 11:15 a.m. (Spanish),
12:30 p.m., and 6:30 p.m.
Daily: 7:00 a.m. (except Saturday), 8:00 a.m., 9:00 a.m., and 12:10 p.m.
Holy Day of Obligation Vigil: 5:30 p.m.
Holy Day of Obligation: 7:00 a.m., 8:00 a.m., 9:00 a.m., and 12:10 p.m.
Confessions: Saturday: 3:15-3:45 p.m.; and after all Masses

Devotions:

Novenas: Daily
Rosary: Daily
Exposition of Blessed Sacrament: Friday and Sunday
Benediction: Wednesday, Friday, and Sunday

Facilities:

Gift Shop
Counseling Center

Languages:

English, Spanish, and Portuguese

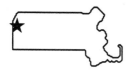

THE SHRINE OF THE DIVINE MERCY

Eden Hill, Stockbridge, Mass. 01262 (413) 298-3931 ext. 174

History of the Shrine:

The Shrine of The Divine Mercy is a popular pilgrimage site known for exquisite wood carvings and stained-glass windows. Erected in thanksgiving to the mercy of God, construction took ten years ending in 1960. The shrine was handcrafted entirely by native people using local materials; funding came from donors throughout the nation. The shrine offices are open daily 9:00 a.m.-5:00 p.m. The pilgrimage season is from the Sunday after Easter to October 31.

The shrine is staffed by the Marians of the Immaculate Conception and is located on 350 acres of land called Eden Hill. The shrine, shrine offices, and gift shop are easily accessible to the disabled.

Schedule of Masses:

Sunday: 10:00 a.m.
Daily: 7:20 a.m.
Saturday: 8:00 a.m.
Holy Day of Obligation: 8:00 a.m.
Confessions: Daily (after the Chaplet of Divine Mercy at 3:15 p.m.)

Devotions:

The Chaplet of Divine Mercy Novena: Daily: 3:15 p.m.
Divine Mercy Sunday: First Sunday after Easter.

Facilities:

Gift Shop, open Monday-Saturday 9:00 a.m.-4:30 p.m.;
Sunday 11:00 a.m.-5:00 p.m.

Languages:

English, Polish, and Spanish

ST. ANNE'S SHRINE

16 Church Street, Sturbridge (Fiskdale), Mass. 01518
(508) 347-7338

**History
of the
Shrine:**

The parish was formed by the union of two missions in 1887. In that year, on the Sunday following the Feast of St. Anne, a parishioner was partially healed of a physical ailment in the church. The following year, on the same Sunday, she was completely healed. Parishioners then gathered at the church and formed the first procession in thanksgiving to God for this favor obtained through the intercession of St. Anne. With that celebration, the shrine was born.

An authentic relic of St. Anne was donated to the Sturbridge shrine in 1893. An outdoor chapel was built, and Sunday Masses began to be celebrated outside. In 1955, Bishop Wright entrusted the care of the shrine to the Assumptionists. In 1971, the Assumptionists brought their unique collection of Russian icons to the shrine for public viewing.

Since that first healing, over one hundred years ago, people have continued to come to this holy place seeking solace and peace from God through the intercession of St. Anne.

**Schedule
of Masses:**

Sunday Vigil: 4:00 p.m. and 6:00 p.m.
Sunday: 8:00 a.m., 10:00 a.m., 12:00 p.m., and 6:00 p.m.
Holy Day of Obligation Vigil: 7:00 p.m.
Holy Day of Obligation: 7:30 a.m., 9:30 a.m., and 7:00 p.m.
Confessions: Saturday: 3:30 p.m. and 7:00 p.m.; and upon request

Devotions:

Novenas: Annually
Anointing of sick: Biannually

Facilities:

Religious Bookstore
Gift Shop
Icon Museum
Outdoor Pavilion
Wheelchair Accessible

Languages:

English, French, and Spanish

SHRINE OF OUR LADY OF GRACE

Route 3 - North, Colebrook, N.H. 03576

History of the Shrine:

This shrine is a monument of love and thanksgiving dedicated to Our Lady for the countless blessings she bestowed upon the Missionary Oblates of Mary Immaculate during their first twenty-five years in Colebrook, N.H.

In the spring of 1948, the Oblates began erecting a monument to the Blessed Lady. The statue of Our Lady was enshrined on September 8 of that year. The Most Rev. Matthew F. Brady, bishop of Manchester, N.H., blessed the main monument on October 10, 1948.

The Way of the Cross was erected and blessed on July 5, 1954 by the Most Rev. Jean-Louis Collignon, OMI, bishop of Les Cayes, Haiti. Each station is a 9-foot granite cross from Stanhope, P.Q. A prayerful atmosphere is enhanced by the fifteen mysteries of the rosary, which are made of carrara marble, barre granite, and fieldstones.

The Oblates of Mary Immaculate had barely come into being when they accepted the direction of the activities of Marian shrines in France. In keeping with the desires of their founder, the Oblates throughout the world have continued the tradition of accepting shrine work. The Shrine of Our Lady of Grace is a seasonal shrine, open from Mother's Day to the second Sunday in October.

Schedule of Masses:

Sunday: 11:00 a.m.
Weekday: 11:00 a.m.
Confessions: Upon request

Devotions:

Sunday Program
Tour of the Shrine: 1:00 p.m.
Way of the Cross: 2:00 p.m.
Rosary, Homily, and Benediction: 3:00 p.m.
Blessing of Motorcycles: Sunday after Father's Day
Triduum: August 12, 13, and 14
Feast of the Assumption: August 15

Facilities:

Gift Shop
Cafeteria

Languages:

English and French

SHRINE OF OUR LADY OF LA SALETTE

Route 4-A, P.O. Box 420, Enfield, N.H. 03748
(603) 632-7087 or (603) 632-4301

History of the Shrine:

Founded in 1951, the Shrine of Our Lady of La Salette, near Lake Mascoma, N.H., is a place of prayer and meditation in a unique, natural setting of peace and beauty. On September 19, 1846, Mary, the Mother of God, appeared to two shepherd children on the slope of a mountain in the French Alps, near the village of La Salette, France. The "Beautiful Lady," as they called her, was seated on a stone, her elbows resting on her knees, her face buried in her hands, weeping bitterly. She rose, calming the children's fear by her reassuring look and maternal voice. She told them the cause of her tears: disobedience to the laws of God and of the Church, blasphemy, failure to keep the Lord's day, and lack of prayer. On the shrine grounds are a replica of the apparition site at La Salette in France, a rosary pond, outdoor Stations of the Cross, the Calvary scene with Holy Stairs, and a peace walk. The shrine is open throughout the year.

The shrine is located in the midst of a historical Shaker Village, and lodging and meals for groups and individuals are available at the adjacent Shaker Inn, which also offers tours of the Shaker Village, Shaker museum, and gift shop.

Schedule of Masses:

Sunday Vigil: 7:30 p.m.
Sunday: 11:00 a.m. (summer season)
Daily: 11:30 a.m. (summer season)
Confessions: 30 minutes before Mass and upon request

Devotions:

Rosary: Sunday: 2:00 p.m. during pilgrimage season

Facilities:

Pilgrim's Chapel
Reconciliation Chapel
Gift Shop
Book Shop
Facilities for Private Retreats

NATIONAL SHRINE OF ST. GERARD

St. Lucy's Church, 118 Seventh Avenue, Newark, N.J. 07104
(201) 482-6663

History of the Shrine:

In 1899, a small group from Caposele, Italy, introduced to the United States, the feast devoted to St. Gerard Majella. This devotion began in St. Lucy's Parish, Newark, N.J., in 1899, five years before Gerard's canonization. The devotion grew steadily throughout the years, and in 1977, St. Gerard's chapel in St. Lucy's Church was dedicated as a national shrine by Archbishop Peter Gerety.

St. Gerard was born in Muro, a small town in the south of Italy, on April 6, 1726. Although he had frail health, he was accepted as a lay brother into the Congregation of the Most Holy Redeemer. During his apprenticeship he performed many miracles, and he is known especially for his "motherhood" miracles. Although he has not been officially designated as the patron of mothers, the title has been given to him by popular acclaim in many countries, including the United States. St. Gerard died in October 1755 at age 29. His feast day is October 16.

Each year during the parish feast days, which includes October 16, there are traditional lights, music, food stands, and processions. Also, the shrine is visited throughout the year by faithful seeking the intercession of St. Gerard.

Devotions:

Wednesday: 5:30 p.m. (Novena and Mass)
Novena and Mass: Nine days prior to the feast day of St. Gerard, October 16: 7:00 p.m.
Anointing of the Sick: On day seven
Blessing of expectant mothers: On day eight
Blessing of all babies born during the year: On day nine
There are processions on the feast day of St. Gerard, as well as on the Saturday and Sunday closest to the feast day. This varies from year to year.

ST. JOSEPH SHRINE

1050 Long Hill Road, Stirling, N.J. 07980
(908) 647-0208

History of the Shrine:

The shrine was founded in 1924 by the founder of Missionary Servants of the Most Holy Trinity, Fr. Thomas Augustine Judge, for devotion to St. Joseph. It has served as a school and a retreat center and is now a place of retreat, pilgrimage, and spiritual refuge. Days of renewal are available for groups of twenty or more. There are no overnight retreats.

The two main celebrations of the year are the feasts of St. Joseph and St. Anthony. There is also a one-week Korean Day Camp for children during the summer.

Schedule of Masses:

Sunday: 8:00 a.m. and 10:00 a.m.
Daily: Monday, Wednesday, Friday, Saturday: 8:00 a.m.; Tuesday, Thursday: 5:30 p.m.
Confessions: Anytime
Holy Day of Obligation: 8:00 a.m. and 10:00 a.m.

Devotions:

Novenas: Annually
Rosary: Daily
Bible Class: Biannually
Novena to St. Joseph: Every Sunday

Facilities:

Religious Bookstore
Gift Shop
Overnight Accommodations (for Religious only)

OUR LADY OF THE ROSARY SHRINE

543 Springfield Avenue, Summit, N.J. 07901
(201) 273-1228

History of the Shrine:

Our Lady of the Rosary Shrine, which is the focal point of devotion at the Monastery of the Dominican Nuns in Summit, N.J., is primarily a sanctuary of prayer. Pilgrims can pay tribute to their eucharistic Lord, exposed day and night for their adoration, and pray the rosary in company with the Mother of Jesus.

On May 22, 1921, a group of pilgrims from Paterson, N.J., traveled to the newly founded monastery of Our Lady of the Rosary where the first outdoor public rosary pilgrimage in the United States took place. On the occasion of the shrine's dedication, Pope Benedict XV sent an apostolic blessing granting a plenary indulgence to all the faithful who would participate in the pilgrimage.

Since that time, the shrine has become widely known and has drawn as many as fifteen thousand pilgrims during the May and October devotions, especially between 1923 and 1934. The privilege of perpetual exposition of the Most Blessed Sacrament was granted to the monastery on February 11, 1926, the Feast of Our Lady of Lourdes.

The monastery is noted for its replica of the Winding Sheet of Turin, which is said to be the cloth in which Our Blessed Lord was wrapped for burial. The replica was fully authenticated and approved by the late Bishop O'Connor of Newark, who authorized its public veneration.

The shrine is staffed by the Dominican Fathers.

Schedule of Masses:

Sunday: 7:30 a.m.
Holy Day of Obligation: 7:15 a.m.

Devotions:

Coronation Pilgrimage: First Sunday of May: 3:00 p.m.
Rosary Pilgrimage: First Sunday of October: 3:00 p.m.
Eucharistic-Marian Hour: Semiannually
Perpetual Adoration of the Blessed Sacrament

Facilities:

Gift Shop

NATIONAL BLUE ARMY SHRINE OF THE IMMACULATE HEART OF MARY

P.O. Box 976, Washington, N.J. 07882 (908) 689-1700

History of the Shrine:

The National Blue Army Shrine of the Immaculate Heart of Mary was built in 1978 in answer to Our Lord's plea to Sister Lucia: "What is being done to spread devotion to the Immaculate Heart of My Mother?" Administered by the Handmaids of Mary Immaculate for the World Apostolate of Fatima in Washington, N.J., the Blue Army represents the fulfillment of the message of Our Lady of Fatima given to the shepherd children in Fatima, Portugal, in 1917.

Celebration of the anniversary of the seven apparitions is held the thirteenth of each month, May through October. All-night vigils are held on the First Friday/First Saturday of each month beginning at 9:00 p.m. and ending Saturday morning.

The shrine is open daily 10:00 a.m.-5:00 p.m. Services are held in the open-air church from May to October.

Schedule of Masses:

Sunday: 11:30 a.m.
Daily: 11:30 a.m.
Latin Liturgy: First Sunday of the Month: 11:30 a.m.
Holy Day of Obligation: 11:30 a.m.
Confessions: 20 minutes before Masses

Devotions:

Novenas: Annually
Rosary: Daily
Benediction: Daily
Exposition: Daily

Facilities:

Religious Bookstore
Gift Shop
Picnic Tables
Outdoor Food Concession Truck (Available on the thirteenth of each month from May to October, and on other major days)
Advance reservations requested for groups of ten or more by car, van, or bus. Write or call for details.

OUR LADY OF MARTYRS

Auriesville, N.Y. 12016
(518) 853-3033

History of the Shrine:

The shrine was built in 1885 on the site of the martyrdoms of Rene Goupil, Isaac Jogues, and John LaLande. It was named after Our Lady of Martyrs with the approval of the Bishops of The Third Council of Baltimore. After the beatification of the Jesuit Martyrs in 1925, it was called the Jesuit Martyrs Shrine.

The main concern of the shrine apostolate is to promote devotion to Our Lady and martyrs. Pilgrims are provided with opportunities for reconciliation, fostering devotion, and strengthening their faith.

Schedule of Masses:

Sunday Vigil: 4:00 p.m.
Sunday: 9:00 a.m., 10:30 a.m., 12:00 p.m., and 4:00 p.m.
Holy Day of Obligation Vigil: 4:00 p.m.
Holy Day of Obligation: 11:30 a.m. and 4:00 p.m.
Daily: 11:30 a.m. and 4:00 p.m.
Confessions: Before Mass each day; priests are available from 10:00 a.m. to 4:30 p.m.

Devotions:

Novenas: Eight held annually
Rosary: Daily after 11:30 Mass
Benediction and Blessing with relics: Daily: 3:30 p.m.
Stations of the Cross: Sunday: 2:30 p.m.

Facilities:

Religious Bookstore
Counseling Center
Gift Shop
Cafeteria
Cultural Center

SACRED HEART DIOCESAN SHRINE

5337 Genesee Street, Route 31, Bowmansville, N.Y. 14026
(716) 683-2375

History of the Shrine:

The present Sacred Heart Diocesan Shrine consists of a large fieldstone shrine one-and-a-half stories high, built by the men of the parish in 1926 (Immaculate Conception portion) and 1927 (Sacred Heart portion), in a park-like setting.

The first (main) part of the shrine is dedicated to the Eucharistic Heart of Jesus and contains three arches designed to recall the Blessed Trinity. A Last Supper scene and a crucifix, both made from Italian marble, recall the institution of the Eucharist. The crucifix depicts a heart on Christ's chest and recalls his Gospel of Love, further given to us through Calvary and each eucharist. Thirty-three steps, representing the number of years of Christ's life, lead above the shrine to a statue of Christ the King; the statue also depicts a heart on his chest.

The second portion of the shrine is dedicated to the Immaculate Conception of the Blessed Virgin Mary. Built in the form of a heart through which the worshipper enters, the shrine contains marble statues of the Annunciation, the apparition at Lourdes, and the Assumption. A fountain, from which water flows down the face of the shrine, recalls the many miracles that occurred at Lourdes through its waters and through faith. At the top rear portion of the heart, an image of the Sorrowful Mother represents the hard aspects of life made bearable through the abundant grace of God, especially as given in his sacraments. (A Man of Sorrows is displayed in the Sacred Heart Shrine.)

The outdoor shrine also contains altars in honor of St. Joseph, St. Anthony, and the Little Flower; there are outdoor Stations of the Cross as well.

Since 1954, one sees over the church altar a statue showing the Lord offering the host and chalice as in the Mass. A special statue, carved for and used during the thirtieth anniversary of the apparitions at Fatima by the same sculptor as the Eucharistic Christ statue, is located at the side altar. Stations of the Cross carved in wood came from Ortiese, Italy; a large carved crucifix came from Oberammergau, Germany. Other carvings at the shrine were created by the Lippich brothers who resided in Bowmansville. A "children's corner" was created with the kneeler, height of artwork, and so forth, designed for use by children only. Fine stained-glass windows stress the missionary character of the church and the time-tested devotions of the Church.

**Schedule
of Masses:**   Sunday Vigil: 6:30 p.m.
                 Sunday: 7:45 a.m., 9:00 a.m., and 12:15 p.m.
                 Holy Day of Obligation: 7:00 a.m., 9:00 a.m., 11:00 a.m., and 6:30 p.m.
                 Confessions: Saturday: 3:30-5:30 p.m. and 7:15-8:00 p.m.; and upon
                 request

Devotions: First Friday Mass and Devotions: 9:00 a.m. and 7:30 p.m., followed by
                 Holy Hour.
                 First Saturday Mass: Early Holy Hour with Mass: 8:00 a.m.

Languages: English

OUR LADY, HELP OF CHRISTIANS SHRINE

4125 Union Road, Cheektowaga, N.Y. 14225 (716) 634-3420

History of the Shrine:

This is truly an immigrant shrine. The family of Joseph Batt left Alsace in 1836. On the voyage across the Atlantic, when a terrible storm snapped the masts of the ship, the Batts urgently begged the immediate assistance of Our Lady, Help of Christians, while the crew chopped the ropes and masts that almost capsized the ship. Joseph promised to build a shrine to Our Lady if the family survived. The craft survived the storm but drifted without sails; the Gulf Stream brought them to the Irish coast.

True to his promise, Joseph built a small shrine in 1853. Additions were made as immigrants learned about the shrine and came to pray for their urgent needs. The oldest shrine in western New York, this shrine continues in popularity, especially on the Solemnity of the Assumption.

The old church once displayed many crutches, canes, and so forth, along the walls, testifying to the many favors received through the intercession of Our Lady, Help of Christians. These were removed to create more room for worshippers before the parish could afford a new church. The Batts lie in the cemetery behind the old church.

Over the altar, the original painting of the shrine pictures Our Lady with the Christ Child looking in concern upon the foundering ship containing the Batts during the storm. Early worshippers knew the shrine by the name "Maria Hilf (Mary Help) zu Cheektowaga, N.Y." The old church is on the National Register of Historic Places.

A large outdoor shrine of fieldstone features a Way of the Cross up to a Calvary scene; several altars are built within this stone structure. A stone sanctuary kept the priest dry during outdoor Masses during inclement weather. A Mother of Sorrows statue contains various personal memorabilia from pilgrims who take off their shoes for the last mile when walking here. At one time, many people walked from a far-off trolley stop to the shrine. A contemporary church features a woodcarving of Our Lady with a ship in her hand; the church also has a very fine organ.

Schedule of Masses:

Sunday Vigil: 4:00 p.m. and 7:00 p.m.
Sunday: 7:00 a.m., 8:30 a.m., 10:00 a.m., and 12:00 p.m.
Holy Day of Obligation: 7:00 a.m., 8:30 a.m., 10:00 a.m., and 12:00 p.m.
Confessions: Saturday: 2:00-3:00 p.m.

Devotions: Miraculous Medal Novena: Wednesday: 9:30 a.m. (old church)

Language: English

NATIONAL SHRINE OF BLESSED KATERI TEKAKWITHA

P.O. Box 627, Fonda, N.Y. 12068 (518) 853-3646

History of the Shrine:

Kateri Tekakwitha, an Indian maiden, was born on the Auriesville, N.Y., side of the Mohawk River to an Algonquin Indian mother and a Mohawk Indian chief. A few years later, a smallpox epidemic took the lives of her mother, father, and brother; it left her with weak eyes and pockmarked skin. In 1666, a French-and-Indian war party from Canada burned down all the Mohawk Indian villages, forcing the Mohawks to move to the Fonda side of the river. Kateri lived there for ten years in a village called Caughnawaga and was baptized a Christian by a Jesuit in 1676.

After conversion, Kateri refused marriage preferring to devote her life completely to the Great Spirit and her people. The abuse she endured for her virtuousness drove her to seek refuge with the Christian Indians in Canada. There she became the first American Indian to take a vow of perpetual chastity. She died there in 1680 at the age of twenty-four. It is documented that, at the moment of death, the pockmarks disappeared from her face.

In 1950, Kateri's village was discovered by a Conventional Franciscan, Fr. Thomas Grassman. He is responsible for excavating what is today the only completely excavated Iroquois Indian village in the country. Fr. Grassman was the shrine's first director, and it was he who saw to the shrine's growth until his death in 1970. The shrine was not considered to be an official place of devotion until Kateri was declared Blessed by Pope John Paul II in 1980. Blessed Kateri is the patroness of peace and ecology.

Schedule of Masses:

Sunday Vigil: 4:30 p.m. (outdoor pavilion)
Sunday: 10:00 a.m.
Daily: 11:30 a.m. (July-September)

Devotions:

Feast Day of Kateri Tekakwitha: July 14

Facilities:

Gift Shop
Retreat House
Nature Trails
Picnic Area

GRAYMOOR CHRISTIAN UNITY CENTER

Garrison, N.Y. 10524 (914) 424-3671

**History
of the
Shrine:**

The center was established and is staffed by the Franciscan Order. The Franciscan Friars of the Atonement are well known for their work in Christian Unity and their missionary efforts around the world. This young community of men and women was founded in the Episcopal Church by Fr. Paul Wattson and Mother Lurana White in 1898 and was received into the Roman Catholic Church in 1909.

The unprecedented move of a group of religious people to be received together into the Catholic Church captured the imagination of people of both faiths. From the Mount of the Atonement, the magazine called *The Lamp* along with the religious radio program, "The Ave Maria Hour," brought the message of unity and a growth in vocations to the new religious order. St. Christopher's Inn, a temporary shelter for homeless men, still attests to the missionary zeal of the founders, and many other ventures soon gave evidence of the spiritual sincerity of the small group of Franciscan Friars and Sisters at Graymoor, Garrison, N.Y., in the Hudson Valley.

Less than a hundred years later, the friars now serve the people of God in Japan, Brazil, England, Italy, Canada, and the United States.

**Schedule
of Masses:**

Sunday: 11:00 a.m.
Holy Day of Obligation: 8:00 a.m. (Community Mass)
Confessions: 9:00 a.m.-9:00 p.m.

Devotions:

Bible Class: Weekly
Retreats: Weekly

Facilities:

Religious Bookstore
Gift Shop
Overnight Accommodations (for retreats only)

OUR LADY OF VICTORY
BASILICA AND
NATIONAL SHRINE

767 Ridge Road, Lackawanna, N.Y. 14218
(716) 823-2490

**History
of the
Shrine:**

Our Lady of Victory National Shrine stands as a source of inspiration on Victory Hill. Under the leadership of Fr. Nelson Baker, who was devoted to Our Lady of Victory, the basilica was constructed in 1921 and was consecrated on May 25, 1926 by Patrick Cardinal Hayes. Two months later, Pope Pius XI elevated the shrine to a minor basilica, the second in the United States.

The architectural splendor of the shrine, which is reminiscent of the great European churches built during the Renaissance, fosters a prayerful atmosphere. The main altar is accented by twisted, red columns of rare Pyrenese marble and a 9-foot, 1,600-pound statue of Our Lady of Victory. The great center dome depicts the Coronation of Our Lady as Queen of Heaven and Earth.

The parish community of Our Lady of Victory welcomes pilgrims and visitors of all faiths.

**Schedule
of Masses:**

Sunday Vigil: 4:30 p.m.
Sunday; 8:00 a.m., 10:00 a.m., 12:00 p.m., and 4:30 p.m.
Holy Day of Obligation Vigil: 7:30 p.m.
Holy Day of Obligation: 7:30 a.m., 9:00 a.m., 12:10 p.m., and 4:30 p.m.
Weekday: 7:30 a.m., 8:30 a.m., and 12:10 p.m.

Devotions:

February 3-11: Novena of Masses for the Sick

Novenas:
March 19: In Honor of St. Joseph
May 16-24: In Honor of Our Lady of Victory
July 8-16: Thanksgiving to Our Lady of Victory
August 7-15: In Honor of Our Lady's Assumption
September 29-October 7: In Honor of Our Lady of Victory
November 1-30: A Month of Special Prayers for the Faithful Departed
December 17-25: In Honor of the Birth of Our Lord
Rosary: Tuesday: 7:00 p.m.
Adoration of the Blessed Sacrament: Friday, 1:00 p.m.-12:00 a.m.

Facilities:

Gift Shop

NATIONAL SHRINE OF OUR LADY OF MT. CARMEL

P.O. Box 868, Carmelite Drive, Middletown, N.Y. 10940
(914) 344-0876

History of the Shrine:

Devotion to Mary under the title of Our Lady of Mt. Carmel began over eight hundred years ago in the Holy Land. From the beginning, the first Carmelites found in Mary a model for their own lives. Mary shared with the Carmelites, and they with the world, her scapular, a symbol of reconciliation.

The Carmelite devotion to Mary is shared with the world and serves to remind us that Mary was the first disciple of Jesus. As the model of Christian life, she is our teacher, a woman of the people who leads us to Christ.

The National Shrine of Our Lady of Mt. Carmel was established in 1940 at the Carmelite Church of Our Lady of the Scapular of Mt. Carmel at 28th Street and First Avenue in New York City. Part of the important work was to supply scapulars to the Armed Forces during World War II. The devotion to Our Lady of Mt. Carmel grew at the shrine, and soon the work included days of reconciliation and workshops devoted to Mary. Thus began a full Marian Center with Masses, novenas, lectures, and study days.

In 1990, the shrine was transferred to Middletown, N.Y., where the beauty of the grounds, a magnificent chapel, and geographic location make it an ideal place for prayer, study, reflection, and pilgrimage. The shrine continues to offer daily and Sunday liturgies, days of recollection, novenas, and celebrations for special Carmelite feast days, rosary processions, sacrament of reconciliation, and spiritual direction. All programs at the National Shrine of Our Lady of Mt. Carmel are conducted in both English and Spanish and promote spirituality of prayer, reflection, meditation, and devotion to Mary.

Schedule of Masses:

Sunday: 12:00 p.m.
Daily: 7:30 a.m. and 11:30 a.m.
Saturday: 8:00 a.m.

Devotions:

Special celebrations and novenas of Masses honoring Our Lady of Mt. Carmel; St. Therese; Carmelite Saints; Infant of Prague, St. Patrick; with Special Liturgies during Advent and Lent.

Facilities:

Renewal Center (for workshops)
Gift Shop

ST. FRANCES CABRINI CHAPEL

701 Fort Washington Avenue, New York, N.Y. 10040
(212) 923-3536

**History
of the
Shrine:**
The chapel was built in 1959 as a shrine for Mother Cabrini's body, which was moved here from Mother Cabrini High School in 1959. The body had been brought to the school chapel in 1933 from West Park, N.Y. In 1938, in the performance of rites necessary for beatification, the body was again exhumed and was transferred to a crystal coffin under the main altar of the sanctuary. On January 11, 1944, Pope Pius XII signed the Decree of Canonization of Blessed Frances Xavier Cabrini.

The remains of Mother Cabrini are enclosed in a glass coffin under the main altar of the chapel. Many visit daily to request graces, favors, and miracles because she has such great favor with God.

Outside groups may arrange to have Mass celebrated in the chapel. The Blessed Sacrament is reserved in an adjoining chapel for those who wish to pray privately. A small photo exhibit depicting St. Cabrini and the works in which her Missionary Sisters of the Sacred Heart have engaged is located in the main lobby of the chapel. Once a month, special novena services are held in her honor. The chapel is open Tuesday through Saturday from 9:00 a.m. to 4:30 p.m.

The most important celebration is the Feast of St. Frances, November 13, which is always celebrated on the second weekend of November.

**Schedule
of Masses:**
Daily: 7:00 a.m.
Sunday: 9:00 a.m. and 11:00 a.m.
Confessions: Before every Mass and the first Sunday of every month
Holy Day of Obligation: 7:00 a.m. and 12:00 p.m.

Activities:
Novenas: Monthly and Annually
Bible Class: Weekly and Monthly
Retreats: Quarterly
Adult and Teenage Retreats
Days of Recollection
Lecture and video on the life of Mother Cabrini

Facilities:
Religious Bookstore
Gift Shop
Mini-Museum of artifacts belonging to Mother Cabrini
Cafeteria

Languages:
English, Spanish, French, and Italian

HOLY INFANT JESUS SHRINE

3452 Niagara Falls Boulevard, North Tonawanda, N.Y.
14120 (716) 694-4313

History of the Shrine:

The Holy Infant Jesus Shrine at Wheatfield, N.Y., was dedicated January 20, 1979, by the Most Rev. Edward D. Head, bishop of Buffalo, N.Y. Transformed from a one-room country school built in 1887, the new shrine replaced the old shrine, which was dedicated by the Most Rev. Aloysius Burke on April 30, 1958.

The Infant Jesus Statue, venerated in the shrine, is a replica of the renowned original statue revered at San Salvatore in Onda Church, in Rome, since the times of St. Vincent Pallotti. This statue symbolizes the immense mercy of God.

The Holy Infant Jesus Shrine is not a parish church. It is a house of prayer and worship, where everyone is free to come, individually or as members of a group or pilgrimage, to pray and celebrate the mysteries of our religion, initiated with the Incarnation of the Son of God.

The specific purpose of the shrine apostolate is the deepening of the awareness that we are adopted sons and daughters of God, extending the image and spirit of Christ in the world.

Schedule of Masses:

Sunday: 11:00 a.m.
Daily: 6:45 a.m.
Thursday: 7:00 p.m.
Holy Day of Obligation: 6:45 a.m.
Confessions: Upon request

Devotions:

Mass, novena to the Infant Jesus, exposition of the Blessed Sacrament with the holy rosary is held every Thursday at 7:00 p.m.
All-Night Vigils (Thursday-Friday) are held on a monthly basis from March to November

Facilities:

Counseling Center

Languages:

English, Polish, Italian, and German

SHRINE OF OUR LADY OF THE ISLAND

Eastport Manor Road, P.O. Box 26, Rockville Centre, N.Y. 11941 (516) 325-0661

History of the Shrine:

In 1953, seventy acres in Eastport, Long Island, were donated to the Montfort Missionaries by Mr. Crescenzo Vigliotta, Sr., for a shrine to honor Mary, Mother of God. In 1957, surrounding acres overlooking Moriches Bay were given to the Missionaries. The shrine officially opened in 1975 with the unveiling of the 25-ton statue of Mary placed on an 18-foot pedestal of rocks facing the Atlantic Ocean. The Blessed Sacrament Chapel was constructed in 1976, followed by the dedication of the shrine in October of that year. Since then, outdoor stations, the rosary walk, pilgrim hall, office building and gift shop, pro-life shrine, *Pieta*, and Shrine to St. Joseph have been added.

Recently, in May 1990, the International Rosary Day was observed at the shrine by a special Rosary Procession, Holy Sacrifice of the Mass, Exposition of the Blessed Sacrament, and Perpetual Rosary. Annually, on August 15, an outdoor Mass is celebrated at 12:00 p.m. followed by a conferral of the Sacrament of the Sick. The sacrament is intended for those afflicted with serious illnesses as well as those who are over sixty years of age.

The shrine has been directed by the Montfort Missionaries over the past sixteen years since the statue of Our Lady arrived.

Schedule of Masses:

Sunday: 10:00 a.m.
Daily: 9:30 a.m.
Holy Day of Obligation: 10 a.m.
Confessions: Upon request

Devotions:

Novenas: Annually
Rosary: Weekly
Immaculate Conception
Blessing of Bikes (Blue Knights)
Divine Mercy Mass: Monthly

Facilities:

Gift Shop
Cafeteria

Languages:

English and French

HOLY DORMITION (ASSUMPTION)

St. Mary's Villa, (Spiritual and Educational Center), RR 1, Box 59, Sloatsburg, N.Y. 10974-9617 (914) 753-5100

History of the Shrine:

The Sisters Servants of Mary Immaculate, a congregation of sisters in the Ukrainian Byzantine Tradition operate and maintain an indoor/outdoor shrine to Our Lady — the Holy Dormition (Assumption).

Visitors are always welcome to the outdoor shrine. The annual pilgrimage takes place on the weekend before the feast of the Dormition (Assumption) of Our Lady with a candlelight procession and service on Saturday evening. Services are in English and Ukrainian.

The indoor shrine welcomes visitors throughout the year for private visits or to join the community in its prayers. The chapel has an icon of the Holy Dormition. The indoor shrine is located within the retreat house setting. It is requested that groups planning to visit the shrine call prior to arrival.

There are no regularly scheduled public Masses at the shrine.

MARIAN SHRINE
NATIONAL SHRINE OF
MARY HELP OF
CHRISTIANS

Filors Lane, West Haverstraw, N.Y. 10993 (914) 947-2200

History of the Shrine:

The Salesians of Don Bosco built a rosary way here in 1954 in observance of the Marian year. Fifteen life-size marble statues, acquired unexpectedly, were placed along a wooded path. People came in increasing numbers to pray along this gospel trail. As the number of pilgrims grew, the shrine was formally established.

Over the years, additional items were added to beautify the Marian shrine. These include the 48-foot bronze Rosary Madonna Statue; the majestic altar of Mary that serves as an outdoor cathedral; grottoes depicting the apparitions at Fatima and Lourdes; the Becchi House (a replica of the home where St. John Bosco grew up); and the large, marble Stations of the Cross.

The shrine is a place for spiritual renewal through pilgrimages and retreats. Although the shrine is open to all, it is particularly geared toward the young. The Salesians strive to make the shrine a place where all can encounter the Lord with the help of Mary. The Blessed Sacrament Chapel is open all day Sunday from 9:00 a.m. to 5:00 p.m. for prayer and meditation.

Spanish Cusillistas, Brooklyn Charismatics, Vigil of Pentecost, Feast of Mary, Help of Christians, Polish Day, and Mount Carmel are some of the celebrations at the Marian Shrine.

Schedule of Masses:

Sunday: 11:00 a.m. and 12:30 p.m.
Daily: 12:00 p.m.
Holy Day of Obligation: 11:00 a.m. and 12:30 p.m.
Confessions: Prior to Mass and upon request

Devotions:

Rosary Procession: Sunday: 3:00 p.m.
Eucharistic Adoration: Sunday: 3:30 p.m.; Wednesday: 8:00 p.m.
Youth Retreats: Tuesdays, Wednesdays, Thursdays, and Fridays (usually adults)
Marriage Preparation: Monthly
Rosary/Eucharistic Devotions: May be scheduled in advance
Prayer phone line

Facilities: Overnight Accommodations and Cafeteria
Religious Bookstore and Gift Shop
Retreat Centers

Languages: Italian, Spanish, French, and Polish

OUR LADY OF FATIMA SHRINE

1023 Swann Road, Youngstown, N.Y. 14174-0167
(716) 754-7489

History of the Shrine:

Through the interaction between the Barnabite Fathers, newly arrived from Italy in 1954, and the people of western New York, this shrine was created and dedicated to the 1917 miracle at Fatima, Portugal, where the Blessed Virgin appeared to three shepherds and asked for prayer and sacrifice so that "Our Lord may save humanity from all calamities and bring peace to the world . . ." She encouraged a simple daily formula for prayer — the rosary — and the need to live the gospel.

In 1962, the Basilica of Our Lady of the Rosary, built in the shape of a globe with a large statue of the Blessed Virgin Mary standing atop it — symbolizing her prayers for the entire world — became the center of the shrine complex, which includes other chapels and facilities as well. The large statue of Our Lady, sculpted from Vermont granite, is over 13-feet high and weighs ten tons. Within the basilica, behind the altar, is the *Peace Mural* that was created by Polish artist Joseph Slawinski in 1975. Within the basilica are two smaller chapels: the Blessed Sacrament Chapel and the Immaculate Heart Chapel. Outside in front of the basilica is a giant rosary circling a heart-shaped pond, and the Avenue of the Saints, lined by over one hundred life-size statues of holy women and men declared Saints of the Church. Also on the grounds are a replica of the first little chapel built at Fatima, Portugal, and the original chapel built here (now englobed in the shrine auxiliary building).

Very special events in the year at the shrine are the Coronation of the Blessed Mother on the second Sunday in August and the Festival of Lights, through the month of December.

Schedule of Masses:

Sunday Vigil: 4:00 p.m.
Sunday: 9:00 a.m., 12:00 p.m., and 5:00 p.m.
Daily: 11:30 a.m. and 4:00 p.m.
Holy Day of Obligation: 9:00 a.m., 12:00 p.m., and 5:00 p.m.
Christmas: 12:00 a.m., 9:00 a.m., and 12:00 p.m.
Easter: 12:00 a.m., 9:00 a.m., 12:00 p.m., and 5:00 p.m.
Thanksgiving: 11:30 a.m.
Reconciliation: Fifteen minutes before liturgies

Devotions:

Novenas: Lent, All Souls, Mother's Day, Father's Day
Rosary and Benediction: Sunday, 3:00 p.m.
Adoration of the Blessed Sacrament: Daily

Facilities: Gift Shop
Cafeteria

Languages: English, French, Spanish, Italian, and Portuguese

NATIONAL SHRINE CENTRE OUR LADY OF GUADALUPE, MOTHER OF THE AMERICAS

501 Ridge Ave., Allentown, Pa. 18102 (215) 433-4404

History of the Shrine:

St. John Neumann founded the first Catholic parish in Allentown, Pa., which he called the Church of the Immaculate Conception of the Blessed Virgin Mary. It was built by Irish immigrants who came here seeking religious freedom.

The church is now the National Shrine Centre and has a steeple that stands 185-feet high. It has some of the finest examples of painted and stained-glass windows made in Germany; sixteen beautiful windows depict the life of the Blessed Virgin Mary. The last window is that of the Sacred Heart of Jesus. On the ceiling are three huge canvasses: The Annunciation, The Immaculate Conception, and The Coronation.

The shrine is on the side altar where the pilgrims can get a close-up view of what is considered the finest reproduction of the Guadalupe picture. It is said "Go to Allentown; if you can't, go to Mexico."

The shrine was dedicated on Saturday, October 5, 1974, by Bishop Joseph McShea, the first bishop of Allentown; Bishop Sidney L. Metzger of El Paso, Texas; Bishop John Venancio of Fatima, Portugal; archabbot of the Basilica of Guadalupe, Guilliamo Schulmberg, and the archpriest of the Basilica of Guadalupe, both of Mexico City.

Schedule of Masses:

Sunday Vigil: 4:15 p.m.
Sundays: 8:00 a.m., 10:30 a.m., and 12:00 p.m.
Daily: 6:30 a.m. and 8:00 a.m.
Holy Day of Obligation Vigil: 6:45 p.m.
Holy Day of Obligation: 8:00 a.m. and 6:45 p.m.
First Friday: 6:30 a.m. and 8:00 a.m.

Devotions:

Novena in Honor of Our Lady of Guadalupe: Monday: 8:00 a.m.
Rosary: 7:45 a.m.

NATIONAL SHRINE OF OUR LADY OF CZESTOCHOWA

P.O. Box 151, Doylestown, Pa. 18901 (215) 345-0600

History of the Shrine:

The National Shrine of Our Lady of Czestochowa was dedicated on October 16, 1966, as a center of Marian devotion. It was built on Beacon Hill in commemoration of the one thousand years of Poland's Christianity. The original barn chapel was used as the main place of worship until the shrine's completion.

The shrine is open throughout the year as a spiritual and cultural center for Americans of Polish descent. There are also pilgrimages of Spanish, Haitian, French, Italian, and Lithuanian apostolates.

The main religious celebration of the year is the Feast of Our Lady of Czestochowa. The average attendance at this celebration is about 6,000. Approximately 500,000 people visit the shrine annually.

Schedule of Masses:

Sunday Vigil: 5:00 p.m.
Sunday: 8:00 a.m., 9:00 a.m., 10:00 a.m., 11:00 a.m., 12:00 p.m., 2:00 p.m., and 5:00 p.m.
Holy Day of Obligation: 7:30 a.m., 8:00 a.m., 11:30 a.m., and 5:00 p.m.
Confessions: Before 11:30 a.m. every day and throughout Sunday

Devotions:

Novenas: Weekly
Rosary: Weekly

Facilities:

Religious Bookstore
Gift Shop
Cafeteria

Languages:

English, Polish, Spanish, French, and Slovak (Korean and Vietnamese groups also visit with their priests.)

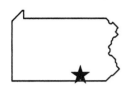

BASILICA OF THE
SACRED HEART OF JESUS

30 Basilica Drive, Hanover, Pa. 17331-8924 (717) 637-2721

History of the Shrine:

The Basilica of the Sacred Heart of Jesus, named a basilica by Pope John XXIII on June 30, 1962, was called the Conewago Chapel in colonial times. The chapel was built in 1741 by Fr. William Wappeler, SJ, a priest sent to minister to the German Catholic immigrants in the area. The chapel was dedicated to St. Mary of the Assumption, but immediately was known as Conewago Chapel.

By 1784, the congregation had grown to over a thousand members, and a new church was constructed and completed in 1787. Sacred Heart of Jesus is the name Fr. Pellentz gave this imposing edifice. It became the first parish church in America dedicated to the loving heart of our Divine Savior and it is the oldest Catholic church building made of stone in the country.

In 1800, the church property was renamed the Conewago Plantation, as it had gradually grown from a Mass station and log chapel to the largest parish in the United States. In 1850, the building was again enlarged by the addition of a transept and apse, under the direction of Fr. Joseph Enders, SJ. Fr. Enders also enlarged the small oratory near the vestibule to serve as a daily chapel. A beautiful painting of the Assumption of Mary was received in 1987, and the chapel was renovated and renamed as Our Lady's Chapel that same year.

The church was turned over to the Diocese of Harrisburg on June 3, 1901.

Schedule of Masses:

Sunday Vigil: 6:30 p.m.
Sunday: 7:30 a.m. and 10:00 a.m.
Weekly: 7:00 a.m. (school days); 8:00 a.m. (other weekdays)
Confessions: Saturday: 4:00 p.m. and 6:00 p.m.; Sunday: 9:30 a.m.
Holy Day of Obligation Vigil: 7:00 p.m.
Holy Day of Obligation: 5:30 a.m., 11:00 a.m., and 7:00 p.m.

Devotions: First Friday: 11:00 a.m. (during school year) and 7:00 p.m.

Facilities: Bus Tours (arranged in advance)

SHRINE OF THE SACRED HEART

Box 500, Harleigh, Pa. 18225 (717) 455-1162

History of the Shrine:

The shrine was founded by Rev. Girard F. Angelo in 1975. Situated in the Harleigh section of Hazleton, Pa., in the Diocese of Scranton, it is the largest outdoor shrine in North America devoted to the Sacred Heart. It is a contemporary reminder of the majesty of the Sacred Heart and a serene embodiment of devotion to him.

The shrine is constructed on a slight incline with five plateaus, each containing a multi-colored geometric walk along which are plaques depicting the Twelve Promises of the Sacred Heart to St. Margaret Mary Alacoque. A winding pathway contains the Stations of the Cross, each made of white Carrara marble set on a granite slab. The focal point of the shrine is the statue of the Sacred Heart, also of Carrara marble. A huge crucifixion scene and a tomb of Christ embedded in the mountainside complete the attractions.

The shrine is open throughout the year. Individuals and groups are welcome.

Schedule of Masses:

Sunday Vigil: 6:00 p.m.
Sunday: 8:00 a.m. and 10:00 a.m.
Confessions: Before each Mass
Holy Day of Obligation Vigil: 7:00 p.m.
Holy Day of Obligation: 8:00 a.m. and 12:00 p.m.

Devotions:

Novenas: Monthly
Rosary: Weekly
Facilities: Religious Bookstore
Overnight Accommodations
Gift Shop
Cafeteria
Cultural Center

Languages:

English and Italian

GROTTO OF OUR LADY OF LOURDES SISTERS OF ST. BASIL THE GREAT

710 Fox Chase Road, Philadelphia, Pa. 19111
(215) 379-2817 or (215) 342-4222

**History
of the
Shrine:**

The first pilgrimage to the Grotto of Our Lady of Lourdes on the grounds of the Sisters of St. Basil the Great was inaugurated by the Very Reverend Mother M. Josaphat Theodorowyck, OSBM, major superior, on Mother's Day, 1938.

A plenary indulgence was granted in 1940 by the Holy See to all faithful who participated in the pilgrimage. Annually, pilgrims primarily from the Ukrainian Catholic parishes attend. All are welcome! The Pilgrimage is held annually on Mother's Day.

**Schedule
of Masses:**

Mother's Day: 9:00 a.m., 10:00 a.m. (communal healing and anointing service), 11:00 a.m. (pontifical divine liturgy), 1:00 p.m., 2:00 p.m. (water blessing at the grotto rosary/blessing of religious articles), 3:00 p.m. (solemn procession to the Grotto Moleben to the Mother of God) Confessions: 8:00-11:30 a.m.

Facilities: Basilian Gift Shop
Cultural Center

Languages: English and Ukrainian

NATIONAL SHRINE OF
ST. JOHN NEUMANN

St. Peter the Apostle Church, 5th Street and Girard Avenue, Philadelphia, Pa. 19123 (215) 627-3080

History of the Shrine:

St. John Neumann, one of the pioneers of the American Catholic Church, was responsible for organizing the diocesan schedule of the Forty Hours Devotion, the establishment of the first system of parochial schools and the first church in America for Italians, and the founding of the Glen Riddle group of the Third Order of the Sisters of St. Francis.

Neumann was born in 1811, in Bohemia, and left his native land to be a missionary in America. In 1836, he was ordained by Bishop John Dubois in New York. Neumann joined the Redemptorists four years later, and was the first to make his religious profession as a Redemptorist in the New World. A decade later he was consecrated fourth bishop of Philadelphia by order of Pope Pius IX.

At forty-eight years of age, exhausted from his endeavors, he died on the street a few blocks from Logan Square, the site of his new cathedral. His remains now repose in the crypt of St. Peter's Church in Philadelphia. Pope Benedict XV said of his remarkable life, "You are all bound to imitate Venerable Neumann." The Vatican Congregation for the Causes of Saints has officially verified that three people are alive today because of the intercession of Bishop Neumann. The miracle in 1963 paved the way for his canonization by Pope Paul VI on June 19, 1977.

The shrine is open daily from 7:30 a.m. to 6:00 p.m. and Sunday from 7:30 a.m. to 5:00 p.m. Pilgrimage Groups are welcome.

Schedule of Masses:

Sunday Vigil: 5:30 p.m.
Sunday: 7:30 a.m., 9:30 a.m., 11:00 a.m. (Spanish), 12:30 p.m., and 3:30 p.m.
Weekday: 7:30 a.m., 12:15 p.m., and 5:30 p.m.

Devotions:

St. John Neumann Novena: Weekday: 12:15 p.m. (with blessing of the sick); Sunday: 3:00 p.m., followed by Mass at 3:30 p.m.
Our Lady of Perpetual Help Novena: Wednesday: 7:00 p.m., prayers at all the Masses on Wednesdays
First Friday: Exposition 1:00-6:00 p.m.
First Saturday: 10:00 a.m. (nuns' holy hour and Mass); 12:15 p.m. (Mass and Fatima vigil until 2:45 p.m.)

Facilities:

Shrine Museum and Exhibit
Gift Shop

ST. ANTHONY'S CHAPEL
THE SHRINE ON
THE HILL

1704 Harpster Street, Pittsburgh, Pa. 15212 (412) 323-9504

**History
of the
Shrine:**

Construction began on the chapel in 1880 under the direction of Fr. Suitbert G. Mollinger, son of a wealthy Belgian family and the first pastor of Most Holy Name of Jesus Church. Fr. Mollinger personally financed the building of the tiny devotional chapel to house his large collection of relics. Dedication of the chapel took place on the Feast of St. Anthony, June 13, 1883. Thousands of people made their way to visit the shrine and to be blessed by Fr. Mollinger and the relic of St. Anthony, the most venerated of all relics in the chapel.

More than five thousand relics of the saints have reposed peacefully in the chapel for more than a hundred years. Among these relics are three central reminders of the most profound aspects of the faith: Christ's suffering and death on the cross, and his glorious resurrection from the dead. A large cross in the center holds a splinter of the True Cross, a thorn from the Crown of Thorns, and a piece of stone from the Holy Sepulchre.

The Chapel of St. Anthony of Padua has been sanctified by the prayers of the faithful for one hundred years. It is hoped that visits to the chapel and prayers through the intercession of The Wonder Worker will enable the good works of St. Anthony to bless the faithful for many years.

The chapel is open on Sundays from 11:00 a.m. to 4:00 p.m.; and Tuesdays, Thursdays, and Saturdays from 1:00 p.m. to 4:00 p.m. It is closed on holidays. Tours may be arranged by calling St. Anthony's Chapel.

**Schedule
of Masses:**

Sundays: 7:30 a.m., 9:00 a.m., and 11:30 a.m.
Daily: 8:30 a.m. (Most Holy Name Church)
Tuesday: 8:30 a.m. (St. Anthony's Chapel)

Devotions:

Novena to St. Anthony: Tuesday: 7:30 p.m.

Facilities:

Religious Bookstore
Gift Shop
Museum

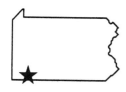

SHRINE OF OUR LADY OF PERPETUAL HELP

510 West Main Street, Box 878, Uniontown, Pa. 15401
(412) 438-7149

**History
of the
Shrine:**
In 1935, Pope Pius XI presented the Sisters of the Order of St. Basil the Great with an Icon of Our Lady of Perpetual Help. This particular icon is a reproduction of the miraculous icon that is venerated in the Church of St. Alphonsus in Rome. In entrusting this icon to the sisters, Pope Pius XI requested that devotion to the Mother of God under the title of Our Lady of Perpetual Help be promoted.

Today, Mount St. Macrina Retreat Center, a ninety-year old mansion, is the location of the Shrine of Our Lady of Perpetual Help. The shrine is staffed by the Sisters of the Order of St. Basil the Great, a Byzantine Rite Community.

Individuals and groups are invited to make day pilgrimages to the shrine. Arrangements can be made by contacting the director of the retreat center.

Each year, during the Labor Day Weekend, a pilgrimage for thousands of Byzantine and Roman Rite Catholics is held on the grounds of Mount St. Macrina in honor of Our Lady of Perpetual Help.

**Schedule
of Masses:**
There are no regularly scheduled Masses, although there are private liturgies for retreat groups.

Devotions:
Since the shrine is located in the retreat center, the center offers various types of retreats, workshops, and days of reflection. The center is also available for anyone seeking quiet and solitude as a respite from their busy schedules, whether for a day or longer. Day pilgrimages to the shrine are also encouraged.

Facilities:
The shrine offers over one hundred acres of natural beauty, dotted with outdoor shrines and chapels for private prayer. The retreat center is an elegant mansion with conference rooms, chapel, and a dining area seating sixty people. There are overnight accommodations for thirty-five people in small dormitory-style rooms. In a nearby annex, there are six semiprivate rooms. There is also a religious gift shop and an icon shop.

Languages:
English and Slavonic

ST. THERESA OF THE CHILD JESUS

7 Dion Drive, Nasonville, Harrisville, R.I. 02830
(401) 568-8280

**History
of the
Shrine:**

It is believed that a parishioner was cured through the intercession of St. Theresa of the Child Jesus in 1923. This is the first shrine in the United States dedicated to St. Theresa. Although small in size, the shrine attracts thousands of people from the New England area, yet it remains a place of refuge and prayer nestled under tall trees on the grounds.

The Feast of St. Theresa of the Child Jesus is celebrated in the shrine on the Sunday closest to October 1.

**Schedule
of Masses:**

Sunday Vigil: 5:00 p.m.
Sunday: 8:00 a.m. and 10:30 a.m.
Daily: 8:30 a.m.
Holy Day of Obligation Vigil: 7:00 p.m.
Holy Day of Obligation: 8:30 a.m. and 7:00 p.m.
Confessions: Saturday: 4:00 p.m.

Devotions: Rosary: Tuesday: 6:30 p.m.

Languages: English and French

ST. ANNE'S SHRINE

Isle La Motte, Vt. 05463
(802) 928-3362

**History
of the
Shrine:**

St. Anne's Shrine nestles close by beautiful Lake Champlain on Isle La Motte. The shrine is situated on the site of Fort St. Anne, Vermont's oldest settlement, constructed in 1666, where the first Mass in Vermont was celebrated. Though the fort itself was short-lived, the site continued to be a favorite stopping place for Lake Champlain travelers in the succeeding years of war and peace.

The shrine is run by the Edmundite Fathers and Brothers and is open from May 15 to October 15. Eucharistic Celebrations are held daily in the open-air pavilion.

**Schedule
of Masses:**

Sunday Vigil: 7:00 p.m.
Sunday: 8:30 a.m., 10:00 a.m., 11:15 a.m., and 4:00 p.m.
Holy Day of Obligation Vigil: 7:00 p.m.
Holy Day of Obligation: 8:30 a.m., 10:00 a.m., 11:15 a.m., and 4:00 p.m.
Confessions: Before all Masses and Devotions

Devotions:

Rosary: Monthly
Novenas: Annually
Retreats: Monthly
Triduum in Honor of St. Anne (July 23 and 26)

Facilities:

Religious Bookstore
Gift Shop
Cafeteria

Languages:

English and French

SOUTH

ST. JOSEPH PROTO-CATHEDRAL

310 W. Stephen Foster Avenue, Bardstown, Ky. 40004
(502) 348-3126

**History
of the
Shrine:**

St. Joseph Proto-Cathedral is the first west of the Allegheny Mountains and is listed by the U.S. Library of Congress as possessing exceptional interest and worthy of careful preservation.

The magnificent structure, completed in 1819, rose in the Kentucky wilderness, a monument to the faith, toil, and zeal of a French priest, Benedict Joseph Flaget, who became the first bishop of Bardstown. This historic edifice contains fine paintings, gifts of Francis I, King of the Two Sicilies, and Pope Leo XII. Other gifts came from the nobles of Europe, including King Louis Phillippe of France.

In 1775, Catholic settlers, mostly of English and Irish descent, began emigrating chiefly from Maryland to Kentucky, an outpost of the crown colony of Virginia. The first missionaries came around 1787. In 1808, the four new Catholic dioceses, created at request of Bishop Carroll of Baltimore, included Bardstown along with Boston, New York, and Philadelphia.

In 1811, three years after he was appointed, Bishop Flaget arrived at Bardstown, traveling down the Ohio River by flatboat and overland from Louisville by wagon, accompanied by a group of seminarians. Bishop Flaget was able to build a small brick church near Bardstown, named St. Thomas. Soon he was consumed with the idea of erecting a cathedral of majestic proportions. Since most of the settlers were very poor, people contributed their materials and their labor as carpenters and masons to build the cathedral. Protestants and Catholics worked together.

After a five-year struggle to get enough money to begin this large undertaking, the cornerstone of the cathedral was laid in 1816. Bricks were baked on the grounds, and solid tree trunks cut from the wilderness were lathed in a circular pattern to form the stately columns supporting the building.

The cathedral was consecrated in 1819, though the interior was not f lly completed until 1823. When the Episcopal See was moved forty miles away to the fast-growing city of Louisville in 1841, St. Joseph's became a parish church, hence, the title "proto-cathedral."

**Schedule
of Masses:**

Sunday Vigil: 5:30 p.m.
Sunday: 7:00 a.m., 9:00 a.m., and 11:00 a.m.
Daily: Monday and Wednesday: 6:30 a.m.; Tuesday, Thursday, and Friday: 7:45 a.m.

SHRINE OF MARY, MOTHER OF THE CHURCH AND MODEL OF ALL CHRISTIANS

434 Church Street, Bowling Green, Ky. 42101
(502) 842-2525

History of the Shrine:

The shrine, blessed on May 7, 1989, by Most Rev. John McRaith, is 35-feet by 15-feet with seating for more than thirty people. Nine stained-glass windows commemorate the following: Cana, Guadalupe, Miraculous Medal, Tri-millennium 2000, Legion of Mary, La Salette, Lourdes, Fatima, and Tre Fontane. Three large windows in the front commemorate the "Miracle of the Sun" at Fatima. On the other side, three large windows commemorate St. Peter, St. Paul, and the Sacred Heart of Jesus.

The Blessed Sacrament is kept at the shrine, and there is a large statue of Mary.

Catholics and non-Catholics alike from this community come virtually daily to pray in the shrine. From time to time there is a pilgrimage from distant parishes.

Schedule of Masses: Mass is offered on First Saturdays.

Devotions: Rosary: Saturdays: 5:00 p.m.
Benediction and Exposition: At various times throughout the year.

SHRINE OF OUR LADY OF GUADALUPE

617 East Main Street, P.O. Box 168, Carlisle, Ky. 40311
(606) 289-5502

History of the Shrine:

The shrine, founded in 1902, was originally known as St. John Church. The church building was constructed in 1906, and a rectory was built next to the church in 1914. The parish struggled to survive during two World Wars and the Great Depression. From 1946 until 1962, it was operated by the Redemptorist Fathers who ran a mission house.

In 1962, Most Rev. Richard H. Ackerman (bishop of Covington), saw the need for a Marian shrine in the diocese. The parish of Carlisle was thus renamed the Shrine of Our Lady of Guadalupe on May 31, 1962. Our Lady of Guadalupe was chosen as patroness because Bishop Ackerman had worked with Hispanic Americans when he was the auxiliary bishop of San Diego in the 1950s. It was hoped that pilgrims would travel to Carlisle to visit their diocesan shrine out of love for Our Lady and, by their generosity, would help the financial plight of the parish through donations.

A new shrine was dedicated on the Feast of the Assumption in 1982, which replaced the original church that had severe structural problems. The shrine has been in the Diocese of Lexington since the new diocese was created in 1988.

The only major celebration of the year is a potluck dinner on the Sunday closest to the Feast of Our Lady of Guadalupe.

Schedule of Masses:

Sunday Vigil: 5:00 p.m.
Sunday: 10:00 a.m.
Confessions: Saturday: 4:15-4:45 p.m.; and by appointment
Holy Day of Obligation Vigil: 5:00 p.m.
Holy Day of Obligation: 7:00 p.m.

CATHEDRAL BASILICA OF THE ASSUMPTION

1140 Madison Avenue, Covington, Ky. 41011
(606) 431-2060

**History
of the
Shrine:**

The Cathedral Basilica of the Assumption, seat of the Catholic Diocese of Covington, Ky., is a living monument to the strenuous labors and ardent faith of those who dared to build this edifice of glass. It is an art and architectural monument to be treasured for centuries by people everywhere.

The building of the cathedral was the lifelong dream of Most Rev. Camillus Paul Maes, third bishop of the Diocese of Covington. The dream evolved into a seemingly interminable project, which was begun in 1894.

The basilica, similar to most of the Gothic cathedrals built in the middle ages, is dedicated to the Blessed Virgin Mary, or "Our Lady" (Notre Dame), celebrating the human vessel by which Christ became man. The figure of The Madonna and Child strikes the beholder as wonderfully lifelike, and compels one to study and to speculate upon the expressive faces of the Mother and the Infant — the infinite love of Jesus, the cooperation of the Blessed Virgin, and the glory of God.

The majestic north transept window, 64-feet wide, presides here as the largest stained-glass church window in the world. The window presents the early fifth-century Ecumenical Council of Ephesus that proclaimed Mary the Mother of God. The supper tier illustrates the Coronation of the Blessed Virgin Mary as queen of heaven and earth. The massive carved Marian shrine depicts the seven joys and the seven sorrows of the Blessed Mother of Jesus.

Pilgrims and visitors are always welcome. Over ten thousand people come on scheduled tours; numerous others come daily to experience the transcendent beauty and presence of God. Parishioners and friends of the cathedral gather on August 15 to celebrate God's goodness and presence among us.

This worthy testimonial of the faith of the people of yesteryear, linked with those who seek a religious awareness of God in today's world, is truly a wonder to behold!

**Schedule
of Masses:**

Sunday Vigil: 5:30 p.m.
Sunday: 10 a.m., 5:30 p.m.
Daily: 7:15 a.m., 12:05 p.m.
Saturday: 12:05 p.m.

Holy Day of Obligation Vigil: 5:30 p.m.
Holy Day of Obligation: 7:15 a.m. and 12:05 p.m.
Reconciliation: At any time

Devotions: Christian Initiation of Adults Program: Weekly
Advent Lessons and Carols: Second Sunday of Advent
Evening Prayer and Speaker: Friday evenings, Lent
Patronal Feastday Celebration: August 15
Concerts of Sacred Music: Monthly on Sunday
afternoons at 3:00 p.m.

Facilities: Accessible to the Disabled
Gift Shop
Museum
Meditation Gardens
Meeting Room

Languages: Some services are signed for the deaf

THE SHRINE OF ST. ANN

St. Ann's Church, 1274 Parkway, Covington, Ky. 41011
(606) 261-9548

History of the Shrine:

Through the efforts of Rev. Louis G. Clermont, relics were secured in 1888 and thus the Shrine of St. Ann was established.

On July 18, 1888, a Novena was started for nine days ending on July 26, the feast of Ss. Ann and Joachim, with a candlelight procession through the West Covington neighborhood.

This tradition continues even today. The shrine draws crowds from all over the Northern Kentucky and Greater Cincinnati, Ohio, area for this novena. Bishop Kendrick Williams (then auxiliary bishop of Covington) celebrated the one hundredth anniversary of the novena on July 26, 1988 with the parishioners of St. Ann and novena participants.

During the nine days of the novena, people can sign up for the St. Ann Pilgrim Society. A donation can be made and a Mass is said every week of the year at the church for all the intentions of the society members.

Schedule of Masses:

Sunday Vigil: 6:00 p.m.
Sunday: 9:30 a.m. (Hathaway Court), 11:00 a.m.
Weekday: 9:30 a.m.

Devotions:

Novena to St. Ann: July 18-26

Facilities:

Accessible to the Disabled

THE SHRINE OF THE LITTLE FLOWER

St. Therese Church, 11 Temple Place, Southgate, Ky. 41071
(606) 441-1654

**History
of the
Shrine:**

In 1927, the Catholic families in the surrounding areas of Southgate, Ky., wanted their own church and school. By the same token, the bishop of the diocese, aware of the needs of his flock, purchased a piece of property on Alexandria Pike in August 1927. The parish had its beginning.

These Catholic families welcomed the opportunity to work many and long hours to ready the old building for occupancy. Bishop Howard canonically erected the parish on August 15, 1927, the great Feast of the Assumption of Our Lady.

Bishop Howard appointed Msgr. Lehr the first pastor. Msgr. Lehr worked side by side with his parishioners to give the new parish a sound foundation to grow and develop.

Enthusiasm intermingled with appreciation became a driving force within the small group to hasten the day of the first Mass in the new church. Using an altar borrowed from the Sisters of the Good Shepherd Convent in Fort Thomas, Ky., the first Mass at the new site was offered by Msgr. Lehr on Sunday, August 21, 1927.

On October 2, 1927, Bishop Howard dedicated the new St. Therese church and school. By the first anniversary of the parish, the growth of the parish had exceeded all expectations. The following day, on the Feast of the Little Flower, Bishop Howard declared the new church a diocesan shrine of the Little Flower. A perpetual novena was inaugurated at this shrine in honor of the Little Flower, as were five annual special novena services.

The reliquary includes three first-class relics of St. Therese, one presented to Msgr. Lehr, and two relics from Bishop Howard, as well as a gift from Mother Agnes when the bishop visited Lisieux in the early fall of 1929.

**Schedule
of Masses:**

Sunday Vigil: 5:00 p.m. (junior choir, first and third Saturdays)
Sunday: 8:00 a.m., 10:15 a.m. (senior choir, first and third Sundays), and 12:00 p.m.
Daily: 7:00 a.m., 8:15 a.m.
Holy Day of Obligation Vigil: 7:00 p.m.
Holy Day of Obligation: 7:00 a.m., 8:15 a.m., 11:00 a.m., and 7:00 p.m.

SHRINE OF ST. JOHN BERCHMANS

*1821 Academy Road, P.O. Box 310, Grand Coteau, La.
70541 (318) 662-5494*

**History
of the
Shrine:**

In 1866, in the little town of Grand Coteau, La., Blessed John Berchmans appeared to a young novice of the Society of the Sacred Heart. Through the intercession of this Belgian, Mary Wilson was miraculously cured of a disease. The Catholic Church, in accepting this miracle, proclaimed John Berchmans a saint of the Church. He is the patron saint of all altar boys in the Church. The infirmary room where the miracle occurred has been converted into a chapel where hundreds come to pray each year. This shrine is the only place in the United States where the exact spot of a miraculous occurrence has been preserved as a shrine.

The Academy of the Sacred Heart, located on the grounds and founded in 1821, is the oldest continuously-operated of the more than two hundred Sacred Heart schools located on five continents around the world.

Tours, lasting about an hour, give the history of the academy, gardens, buildings, shrine, and locations of Civil War battles. The academy and shrine are listed on the National Historical Register.

**Schedule
of Tours:**   Only upon request

Facilities: Museum
Gardens

Languages: English and French (upon request)

ST. ANN NATIONAL SHRINE

4920 Loveland Street, Metairie, La. 70006
(504) 455-7071

**History
of the
Shrine:**

St. Ann Church and Shrine, originally designated as St. Ambrose Parish, was founded March 1, 1971. Since the National Shrine to St. Ann was to be erected behind the church, the parish was renamed in honor of St. Ann. The church and shrine as it now stands was completed in October 1976 and was officially dedicated by Archbishop Philip M. Hannan on July 24, 1977.

The stained-glass windows in the body of the church, designed in the form of a cross, represent the Joyful, Sorrowful, and Glorious mysteries of the rosary. The chapels are designated as Our Lady's Chapel, Crucifixion Chapel, and Resurrection Chapel.

The grotto-like structure in the center of the shrine contains the holy stairs which one ascends on his knees while meditating on the Stations of the Cross depicted in the beautiful stained-glass window. Upon reaching the top of the stairs, one finds a large wood-carved crucifix with the statue of St. Ann. The window facing the north depicts St. Ann, the grandmother of Our Savior, and her husband, St. Joachim. These windows are a memorial to the Louisiana Oyster Industry, the fishermen and their families who generously contributed to the building and maintenance of these beautiful windows.

**Schedule
of Masses:**

Sunday Vigil: 4:00 p.m. and 5:30 p.m.
Sunday: 8:00 a.m., 9:30 a.m., 11:00 a.m., 12:15 p.m., and 5:00 p.m.
Daily: 6:30 a.m., 7:30 a.m. (Saturday), 8:30 a.m. (Monday-Friday), 7:30 p.m. (Tuesday).
First Friday: 6:30 a.m., 8:30 a.m. and 11:15 a.m.
Confessions: Saturday: 3:00-4:00 p.m., 4:45-5:30 p.m.; Thursday before First Friday: 7:30 p.m.

Devotions:

Novena to St. Ann: Tuesday: 7:30 p.m.
Exposition of the Blessed Sacrament: 8:30-11:15 a.m. (First Friday)

Facilities:

Gift Shop

INTERNATIONAL SHRINE OF ST. JUDE

Our Lady of Guadalupe Chapel, 411 North Rampart Street,
New Orleans, La. 70112 (504) 525-1551

History of the Shrine:
Ecclesiastical permission for the shrine was obtained in 1935, after a group of parishioners had petitions granted through the Apostle's intercession. The first solemn novena to St. Jude was inaugurated on January 6, 1935. A small statue and a relic of the Apostle Jude were originally placed in a niche in the chapel; as devotions increased, a life-size statue was purchased and was placed in the shrine to the left of the main altar.

The chapel itself is the oldest surviving church in New Orleans and is located on the edge of the historic French Quarter. Built during the yellow-fever epidemic of 1827, the chapel was first used as a mortuary chapel of the cathedral church. In 1865, the chapel provided a gathering place for Confederate veterans. In 1918, care of the chapel was entrusted to the Oblates of Mary Immaculate. The shrine also serves as the memorial chapel for the New Orleans police and fire departments.

Since the first St. Jude devotions in 1935, thousands of people have passed through the doors of the chapel or have attended the solemn novena, seeking the intercession of the apostle known for difficult and apparently impossible cases.

In addition to the Sunday novena to St. Jude, a nine-day solemn novena is held quarterly (during late January, April, July, and October).

Schedule of Masses:
Sunday Vigil: 4:00 p.m.
Sunday: 7:30 a.m., 9:30 a.m., 11:30 a.m., and 6:00 p.m.
Confessions: 30 minutes before Mass and by appointment

Devotions:
Weekly Novena Prayers (after Sunday Masses)
Quarterly Solemn Novenas
Rite of Christian Initiation for Adults
Stations of the Cross (during Lent)
Weekly, Tri-state Radio Broadcasts (daily during Novenas)

Facilities:
St. Jude Hall
St. Jude Community Center
Gift Shop

Languages:
English and Spanish

NATIONAL VOTIVE SHRINE OF OUR LADY OF PROMPT SUCCOR

2635 State Street, New Orleans, La. 70118 (504) 866-1472

History of the Shrine:

History books do not record Mary's role in protecting New Orleans in the battle fought there in 1815. For Catholics of that city, however, it is a well-remembered fact; yearly on January 8, a Mass of Thanksgiving is offered on the anniversary of what is called the Battle of New Orleans.

On the morning of January 8, 1815, the vicar-general celebrated Mass on the main altar, above which the statue had been placed. Before the end of Mass, a messenger arrived to announce the end of the battle and the defeat of the British. The battle had lasted less than twenty minutes.

History records that General Jackson went in person to the convent to thank the nuns for their prayers. According to the Ursulines, this was the second time that Our Lady of Prompt Succor had interceded on behalf of New Orleans. In 1812, when a fire was ravaging the city and the wind was driving the flames toward the Ursuline Convent and the nearby buildings, one of the sisters, before fleeing from the cloister, placed a small statue of Our Lady of Prompt Succor on a windowsill facing the fire. At the same time, another sister prayed aloud: "Our Lady of Prompt Succor, hasten to our help or we are lost." Scarcely had she uttered the last word when the wind changed direction and the convent and environs were saved. Witnesses attest to this fact.

The Ursulines came to New Orleans in 1727, under the auspices of King Louis XV of France, to teach the children of the colonists and to nurse the sick in a hospital. The statue of Our Lady of Prompt Succor was brought from France by one of the sisters in 1810. In fact, it was this holy nun, Mother St. Michel, who had given Mary this title when she had received a speedy answer to her prayers. Before coming to New Orleans, Mother St. Michel had the special statue made, and she promised Our Lady to have her honored in New Orleans under that title.

Pope Pius V authorized the celebration of the feast of Our Lady of Prompt Succor as well as the signing of the yearly Mass of Thanksgiving on January 8. In 1894, Pope Leo XIII issued a decree granting the "Solemn Coronation of the Miraculous Statue of Our Lady of Prompt Succor, exposed to public veneration in the chapel of the Ursuline Convent, New Orleans."

With the approval of the Holy See, the bishops of the Diocese of Louisiana, in June 1928, chose Our Lady of Prompt Succor as Patroness of the City of New Orleans and of the State of Louisiana and designated

January 8 as the patronal feast. The statue is venerated in the National Shrine of Our Lady of Prompt Succor where countless favors have been reported.

Schedule of Masses: Sunday: 9:30 a.m.
Daily: 6:40 a.m. (Monday, Wednesday, and Friday); 5:30 p.m. (Tuesday and Thursday); 11:30 a.m. (Saturday)

Devotions: Peace Mass with Rosary and Confessions: Monthly 6:00-9:30 p.m.
Passio Domini with Benediction: 9:00 a.m.-12:00 p.m. (first Thursday)
Christmas Novena
Feast of Our Lady of Prompt Succor Novena
Solemn Mass of Thanksgiving on January 8, Feast of Our Lady of Prompt Succor

ST. ROCH CHAPEL AND THE CAMPO SANTO

1725 St. Roch Avenue, New Orleans, La. 70117
(504) 945-5961

**History
of the
Shrine:**
St. Roch was born in 1295 in Montpellier, France. Deeply religious, he went to Rome and devoted himself to caring for those stricken by the Black Plague. It is said that through his prayers, Rome was spared from the plague. He returned to Montpellier after seven years but was accused of being a spy and was sent to prison for five years. He died there, and it is said a bright light shone around him at the time of his death. Many miracles have occurred attesting to his sanctity; he is known as the saint to invoke in cases of affliction, disease, and deformities.

In 1867, in New Orleans, Fr. Thevis of Holy Trinity Church appealed to St. Roch that his parishioners be spared during an outbreak of yellow fever. Supposedly, none of them died, so Fr. Thevis fulfilled his promise of erecting a chapel and cemetery in honor of the saint. On September 6, 1875, the cemetery (Campo Santo) was dedicated, and the cornerstone of the chapel was laid. The chapel and shrine were dedicated on August 16, 1876, feast of the saint. People began to flock to the site, especially on his feast day, All Saints Day, All Souls Day, and Good Friday.

Many have attested to being cured through the intercession of St Roch. In a little room to the side of the chapel sanctuary lies a collection of crutches and braces — objects that graphically express the thanks of clients of St. Roch for favors obtained.

**Schedule
of Masses:**
Every Monday morning

Devotions:
Feast of St. Roch: August 16 (Services are held for nine days before his feast)
Good Friday: Way of the Cross, Stations of the Cross (3:00 p.m.)
All Saints Day: Pilgrimage to Campo Santo, Way of the Cross

NATIONAL SHRINE OF THE INFANT JESUS OF PRAGUE

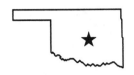

P.O. Box 488, Prague, Okla. 74864 (405) 567-3080

History of the Shrine:

The National Shrine of the Infant Jesus of Prague was dedicated in 1949. This shrine resembles the original shrine located in Prague, Czechoslovakia.

The original statue of the Infant Jesus of Prague was under the care of the Carmelites. Most of the Catholic churches were taken over by the enemy in 1653, and the statue of the Divine Infant was thrown behind the altar. Both hands were broken off the statue. It lay there for seven years, until a priest from Munich discovered the broken statue and began to work for the restoration of the devotion.

The town of Prague, Okla., was organized in 1902 by a group of Czechoslovakian Catholics. Prague was served for many years by various missionaries in a small wooden church. As the town grew, however, it demanded a larger church. In June 1909, Bishop Meerschaert dedicated the new church, St. Wenceslaus, which was destroyed in 1919 by a tornado. In 1948, Fr. George V. Johnson came to Oklahoma on a mission — to build a new church for St. Wenceslaus parish.

Due to the lack of donations, Fr. Johnson was discouraged. He began praying to the Infant of Prague and, shortly afterwards, the new church flourished. Pope Pius XII granted permission to build the National Shrine to the Infant Jesus of Prague. On February 22, 1949, the shrine was dedicated in the modest church of St. Wenceslaus by Bishop McGinnis. A piece of the manger of Bethlehem and the True Cross are found at the shrine. These serve to bring the spiritual nearness of the Little King to the hundreds of pilgrims and tourists who visit the shrine each year.

Schedule of Masses:

Sunday Vigil: 7:30 p.m.
Sunday: 11:00 a.m.
Holy Day of Obligation: 7:00 a.m. and 7:30 p.m.

Devotions: Novenas to the Infant Jesus of Prague: Monthly

Facilities: Gift Shop

SHRINE OF OUR LADY VIRGIN OF THE POOR

New Hope, Tenn. (615) 837-7068

**History
of the
Shrine:**

The Shrine of Our Lady Virgin of the Poor is a replica of the original shrine in Banneaux, Belgium, which marks the site of a 1933 apparition of Mary. This shrine is the creation of Fr. Basil Mattingly, a Benedictine monk.

Mary appeared eight times in Banneaux, between January and March, to Marietta Beco, an 11-year old peasant girl. Mary asked that a little chapel be built in her honor and that people would come and pray in procession, especially the rosary. She called herself the Virgin of the Poor. A small chapel was built beside a spring that appeared during one of the apparitions, and it was blessed August 15, 1933. Bishop Louis J. Kerkofs of Liego gave his approval to devotion to Our Lady of Banneaux in 1949.

While more than one hundred sanctuaries throughout the world are dedicated to Our Lady of Banneaux, Our Lady Virgin of the Poor is the only one in the United States. The shrine itself is small and simple, as Mary requested. It is almost identical to its Belgian model, but the materials are distinctly from the Tennessee area. The stone for the walls and massive altar came from a nearby quarry, and the iron gates were designed and built by a local ironworker.

People from all over the Chattanooga area visit this shrine, with some traveling from Nashville, Alabama, and Georgia, to be renewed and spiritually refreshed.

**Schedule
of Masses:**

Sunday: 7:30 a.m. and 2:00 p.m. (May-October)

LA PURISIMA SHRINE

328 South Nevarez, El Paso, Tex. 79927
(915) 859-7718

History of the Shrine:

This shrine originated in 1840. Neither the designer nor the builder is known. La Purisima takes its name from Socorro, N.Mex., from which the Piro Indian refugees fled to escape the massacre in the 1680 Pueblo revolt.

The building is constructed of adobe, thick-walled and plastered. The flat roof is supported by carved cottonwood and cypress beams.

The two important events of the year are the Feasts of the Immaculate Conception and of St. Michael. The shrine is staffed by the Marist Order.

Schedule of Masses:

Sunday Vigil: 7:00 p.m.
Sunday: 7:30 a.m., 10:30 a.m., and 12:00 p.m.
Holy Day of Obligation: 7:00 p.m.
Confessions: During office hours

Languages: Spanish

NATIONAL SHRINE OF THE LITTLE FLOWER

906 Kentucky Avenue, P.O. Box 5280, San Antonio, Tex. 78201 (512) 735-9126

History of the Shrine:

The National Shrine of the Little Flower serves as a parish church for two thousand Roman Catholics. It was built and is directed by the Discalced Carmelite Fathers. The shrine's massive exterior is made from Indiana limestone; the front is flanked by two massive towers, one of which contains six bells which weigh a total of eight thousand pounds. Centered above the middle of the shrine is a dome 32 feet in diameter and rising to a height of 70 feet.

The Carmelites arrived in this country early this century after being exiled after the bloody battle for Torreon during the revolution. They first became established in Oklahoma and, in 1923, were asked by the archbishop of San Antonio to establish a parish there and to give his people spiritual help. With some difficulties, the Carmelites finally dedicated a church there on August 29, 1926. This building was used to celebrate Mass for the next two years.

In 1927, a plan for the Shrine of St. Therese was conceived. Archbishop Drossaerts gave the Carmelite Fathers his blessing, and the order began its campaign for funds for the new church. People from every part of the world responded to their appeal and, in the fall of 1931, the present building was dedicated to St. Therese by the Most Rev. José Jesus Manriquez, bishop of Huejtla, Mexico.

The shrine contains many different altars, stained-glass windows, paintings, and chapels.

Schedule of Masses:

Sunday: 8:00 a.m., 9:30 a.m., 11:00 a.m., 12:30 p.m., and 5:30 p.m. Weekday: 6:00 a.m., 8:15 a.m. (8:00 a.m. during summer), and 5:30 p.m. Saturday: 8:00 a.m. and 5:30 p.m.

Devotions:

Feast Day of St. Therese: October 1 (Mass)
Novena of Special Prayers: September 20-29
Solemn Triduum: September 29-30, October 1
Feast of St. Teresa of Avila: October 15 (Mass)
St. John of the Cross: December 14 (Mass)

Languages: English and Spanish

VIRGEN DE SAN JUAN SHRINE

400 North Nebraska, P.O. Box 747, San Juan, Tex. 78589
(512) 787-0033

History of the Shrine:

The history of the Virgen de San Juan Shrine has its roots in the religious experience of a people who have felt the very close presence of Mary, the Mother of God. In 1623, through Mary's intercession, a young girl was brought back to life. Mary then became known as La Virgen de San Juan de los Lagos. This story filled the Mexican town with deep feelings of thanksgiving and confidence to La Virgen who took such great care of them.

In 1949, Fr. José Maria Azpiazu, OMI, aware of the devotion of the Mexican Americans to Mary, placed a replica of the statue of La Virgen de San Juan de los Lagos in his parish church of St. John the Baptist. As the number of pilgrims grew, Fr. José decided to build a shrine, which was officially dedicated on May 2, 1954.

The original shrine was destroyed in 1970 as a result of a plane crash. On April 19, 1980, a new, spacious, and modern shrine, able to seat two thousand visitors, was dedicated. Projects now under contract include a 40-foot by 30-foot Italian mosaic, and life-size bronze stations of the cross will be placed on an outside walk. Both projects are to be completed by June 1993.

Schedule of Masses:

Sunday: 6:30 a.m., 8:30 a.m., 10:30 a.m., 12:30 p.m., and 5:30 p.m.
Holy Day of Obligation: 6:30 a.m., 9:30 a.m., 11:30 a.m., and 5:30 p.m.
Confessions: Available throughout the day

Devotions:

Feast of Our Lady: Jan. 25-Feb. 2
Assumption of Our Lady: Aug. 7-15
Mother's Day
Father's Day
All Souls
Rosary: Weekly

Facilities:

Religious Bookstore
Overnight Accommodations
Cafeteria
Retreat House

Languages:

English and Spanish

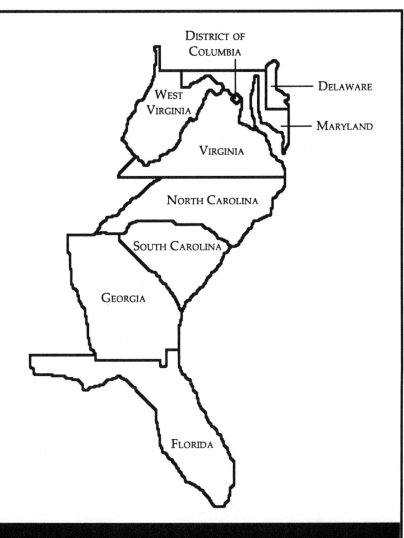

DISTRICT OF
COLUMBIA

WEST
VIRGINIA

DELAWARE

MARYLAND

VIRGINIA

NORTH CAROLINA

SOUTH CAROLINA

GEORGIA

FLORIDA

SOUTHEAST

ST. FRANCIS XAVIER

(Old Bohemia) Warwick, Md.
c/o St. Joseph's Church,
15 W. Cochran St., P.O. Box 196,
Middletown, Del. 19709 (512) 378-1939

**History
of the
Shrine:**

In 1704, the Jesuits founded St. Francis Xavier as the center for new mission activity east of the Chesapeake Bay. The original boundaries of the parish included the present Diocese of Wilmington and the Archdiocese of Philadelphia.

After the parish seat was moved to Middletown, Del., in 1908, St. Francis Xavier was continued as a mission, but after 1929 only annual field Masses were celebrated at Old Bohemia.

Following World War II, an upsurge of interest in the pioneer parish of the Wilmington diocese led to the formation of the Old Bohemia Historical Society, which restored and now maintains the old church as a historic shrine for the diocese. It commemorates the missionary spirit of St. Francis Xavier and his Jesuit successors, who first planted the seeds of faith within the bounds of the present Diocese of Wilmington.

**Schedule
of Masses:**

First Sunday of April, May, September, and October at 4:00 p.m. (When Easter falls on the fourth Sunday as in 1992, the April pilgrimage is held on the fifth Sunday.)

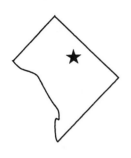

BASILICA OF THE NATIONAL SHRINE OF THE IMMACULATE CONCEPTION

Fourth Street and Michigan Avenue, N.E., Washington, D.C. 20017-1566 (202) 526-8300

History of the Shrine:

The Basilica of the National Shrine is the largest Roman Catholic church in the United States and one of the largest churches in the world. The idea of a national shrine was first conceived in the early 1900s by Bishop Thomas J. Shahan, the fourth rector of The Catholic University of America. Under his direction, the crypt church was completed and the foundation begun; however, because of the Great Depression, financial contributions ceased and all construction came to a standstill. Thus, the project of building the shrine would lay dormant for almost twenty-five years before being revived.

After World War II, Archbishop John Noll of Fort Wayne, Ind., and Archbishop Patrick O'Boyle of Washington, D.C., began to rekindle the dream of the shrine. In 1953, they gained the support of the U.S. Catholic bishops, who then elicited and received funds from every parish in the country as well as from the Knights of Columbus. Construction then resumed in 1954 and, by 1959, the great upper church was completed and dedicated.

The Basilica of the National Shrine, designed in the Byzantine-Romanesque style, contains 57 chapels displaying a wide variety of stained glass, mosaics, and sculpture. Each chapel and piece of artwork in the shrine encompass the history of Catholic devotion to Mary. The shrine is unique among all others in the country because it is the national church for all Catholics who come each year to honor Mary and to renew their faith through worship to God.

The shrine is open from 7:00 a.m.-6:00 p.m., November 1-March 31, and from 7:00 a.m.-7:00 p.m., April 1-October 31.

Schedule of Masses:

Weekday: 7:00 a.m., 7:30 a.m., 8:00 a.m., and 8:30 a.m. (great upper church); 12:10 and 5:15 p.m. (crypt church)
Sunday: 5:15 p.m. (Vigil), 9:00 a.m., 10:30 a.m., 12:00 p.m., and 4:30 p.m. (great upper church); 7:30 a.m., and 1:30 p.m. (crypt church)
Holy Day of Obligation Vigil: 5:30 p.m.
Holy Day of Obligation: 7:00 a.m., 7:30 a.m., 8:00 a.m., 8:30 a.m., 10:00 a.m., 12:00 p.m., and 5:30 p.m.

Confessions: Monday-Saturday: 7:45-8:15 a.m., 10:00 a.m.-12:00 p.m., 3:30-6:00 p.m.; Sunday: 10:00 a.m.-12:00 p.m.

Devotions: Rosary: Weekday: 11:50 a.m. and 4:50 p.m.; Sunday: 1:10 p.m.

Facilities: Gift Shop
Cafeteria
Guided Tours

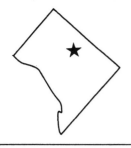

FRANCISCAN MONASTERY (HOLY LAND OF THE AMERICAS)

1400 Quincy Street, N.E., Washington, D.C. 20017
(202) 526-6800

History of the Shrine:

The Franciscans have a long history in the Holy Land as guardians of the Holy Sepulchre. They witnessed firsthand the importance of pilgrimages to the Holy Land in keeping the faith alive. The order was then given the privilege of establishing a shrine to Our Lord, reproducing many of the sites associated with his life, in Washington, D.C.

The monastery/shrine was founded by Fr. Godfrey Schilling, OFM, in the late 1800s and opened to pilgrims in 1898. He named the shrine the Holy Land of the Americas, which it is still called today. The shrine is for the benefit of those who are unable to visit the sacred shrines in the Holy Land. Many shrines and grottoes in the church have been faithfully reproduced according to the originals. These include the Holy Sepulchre, the Sanctuary of Calvary, the Grottoes of Nazareth and Bethlehem, and the Martyrs Crypt. Outdoor shrines include the Valley and Grotto of Gethsemane, the Tomb of the Blessed Virgin, and the Lourdes Grotto.

The church was constructed in the Byzantine style. The main structure of the church contains a large cross, fifteen chapels, and many smaller crosses. The emblem of the five-fold cross, representing the five wounds of Christ, is found throughout the church, thereby establishing its connection to the Holy Land.

The main religious celebrations are Christmas, Holy Week, Easter, and the Feasts of St. Francis and St. Anthony of Padua. About sixty thousand pilgrims visit the shrine annually.

Schedule of Masses:

Sunday Vigil: 5:00 p.m.
Sunday: 7:00 a.m., 8:30 a.m., and 10:30 a.m., 12:00 p.m. and 4:30 p.m. (Spanish)
Holy Day of Obligation Vigil: 5:00 p.m.
Holy Day of Obligation: 6:00 a.m., 7:00 a.m., 8:00 a.m., and 9:00 a.m.
Confessions: Daily 9:00 a.m., 10:00 a.m., 11:00 a.m., 1:00-4:00 p.m.; Sunday 1:00-4:00 p.m.

Devotions:

Novenas: Weekly (St. Anthony)

Facilities: Snack Bar
Gift Shop
Religious Bookstore

Languages: Spanish, Italian, French, Arabic, Polish, and German

UKRAINIAN NATIONAL SHRINE OF THE HOLY FAMILY

4250 Harewood Road, N.E., Washington, D.C. 20017
(202) 526-3737

History of the Shrine:

Our Holy Family Ukrainian Catholic Church, with the help of 210 Catholic parishes in the United States, built this shrine to commemorate the millennium of Christianity among the Ukrainian people. The icons of the Blessed Virgin Mary of Pochayiv are revered in the shrine and grotto. The grotto also contains a 70-foot cross.

Devotion has been paid to the traveling icon of Pochayiv in the parish since 1977, and pilgrimages began in 1980. The shrine caters to special groups — school children, youth groups, senior citizens — as well as to individuals, of any denomination.

Schedule of Masses:

Sunday: 9:30 a.m. (English), 11:15 a.m. (Ukrainian)
Saturday: 9:00 a.m. (English)
Weekdays: 8:00 a.m. (English)
Confessions: Upon request

Devotions:

Prayer Services: Devotion to Pochayiv
Missions
Retreats

Languages: English and Ukrainian

SHRINE OF OUR LADY OF CHARITY

3609 South Miami Avenue, Miami, Fla. 33133
(305) 854-2404 or 2405

History of the Shrine:

The shrine was commissioned by Archbishop Coleman F. Carroll of Miami who asked the Cuban people to build a shrine to honor their patroness. A statue of the Virgin, found in the Bay of Nipe in Cuba at the beginning of the seventeenth century, was to be placed in the shrine. In 1967, a small chapel was erected which was to serve as a convent for the Sisters of Charity who work at the shrine.

The present building stands 90-feet high with a width of 80 feet. Built in the shape of a mantle, the temple invites people to enter within the heart of the Virgin so that they may find the Word of God that lives there.

The statue of Our Lady holding out Jesus in her hands is an invitation for the faithful to enter into communion with him through the sacraments of penance and the eucharist.

This newest Marian shrine in the United States was designed and built by Cuban refugees. John Cardinal Krol of Philadelphia dedicated it on December 2, 1973. The shrine stands as a monument to the religious faith of the Cuban people and their commitment to freedom.

Pilgrimages of members of the 126 Cuban municipalities are scheduled throughout the year as well as six picnics for the six Cuban provinces. The month of October is dedicated to the different advocations of the Blessed Mother and to the people of South and Central American nations who live in the area. Mass each evening is dedicated to one nation. September 8 is the main feast celebrated at the shrine.

Schedule of Masses:

Sunday Vigil: 8:00 p.m.
Confessions: At any time
Holy Day of Obligation Vigil: 8:00 p.m.
Holy Day of Obligation: 8:00 p.m.

Devotions:

Rosary: Daily
Bible Class: For adults by correspondence
Christian Initiation Program for Adults: Weekly
Feast of Our Lady of Charity: September 8

Facilities:

Counseling Center

Languages:

Spanish, English, and French

MARY, QUEEN OF THE UNIVERSE SHRINE

8300 Vineland Avenue, Orlando, Fla. 32821
(407) 239-6600

**History
of the
Shrine:**

The influx of visitors to Orlando from all over the world made it necessary to provide a place of worship for faithful believers, who wanted in particular to celebrate the Eucharist.

In 1975, Fr. F. Joseph Harte began a tourist ministry with Masses in local hotels. In time this ministry blossomed into a shrine honoring Mary, Queen of the Universe.

In 1984, the shrine was commissioned by Bishop Thomas J. Grady of Orlando, and the preliminary structure opened to the public on April 2, 1986. In late November of that year, papal Pro-Nuncio Pio Laghi together with the bishops of Florida officially blessed the new shrine.

Work continues on the new main shrine church, which stands along Interstate 4 near Walt Disney World. The church is expected to be opened before Easter 1993.

A feature of the shrine is the magnificent Mother and Child Outdoor Chapel. The statuary sculpted by the renowned artist Jerzy Kenar stands in tribute to the Incarnation and as a beautiful reminder of the gift of life. Tranquil grounds and flowing fountains complete the prayerful atmosphere of the shrine.

With its main emphasis on evangelization, the shrine will have upon completion a chapel of daily adoration and will provide opportunities for prayer and reconciliation for all who visit the area.

The shrine celebrates its name day on August 22, Feast of the Queenship of Mary.

**Schedule
of Masses:**

Sunday Vigil: 6:00 p.m.
Sunday: 7:30 a.m., 9:30 a.m., 11:30 a.m., and 6:00 p.m.
Daily: 8:00 a.m.
Confessions: Daily

SHRINE OF OUR LADY OF LA LECHE

P.O. Box 3845, St. Augustine, Fla. 32085
(904) 824-2809

History of the Shrine:

In or about 1620, the early Spanish settlers established the first shrine ever in the United States to be dedicated to the Blessed Virgin Mary as a sign of their love for the Nursing Mother of Christ. They did so on the very spot where the first parish Mass had been offered by Fr. Francisco Lopez de Mendoza Grajales, fifty-five years before at the Mission of Nombre de Dios in St. Augustine. The original chapel and several others built after it were destroyed by gunfire during the colonial days and later by hurricanes. The present chapel was begun in 1915 and enshrines a replica of the original statue. The original shrine and statue in the Church of San Luis in Madrid were destroyed during the Spanish Civil War.

Thousands of mothers visit the shrine every year to ask for the blessings of motherhood, beseeching the intercession of Our Lady of La Leche that God will grant them a safe, happy delivery and healthy, holy children.

The principal memorials are the Prince of Peace Church; an 11-foot bronze statue of Fr. Lopez; a 208-foot stainless steel cross; a rustic altar; and a gift shop.

The annual pilgrimage Mass is celebrated at the outdoor altar on September 8, the feast of Our Lady's Birthday. This is also the official date of the founding of the Mission of Nombre de Dios and the City of St. Augustine.

Schedule of Masses:

Sunday Vigil: 6:00 p.m.
Sunday: 8:00 a.m.
Confessions: Following evening Mass
Holy Day of Obligation: 8:30 a.m.

Devotions:

Novenas: Monthly
Rosary: Monthly

Facilities:

Religious Bookstore
Gift Shop
Church Supplies

ST. JUDE SHRINE

309 N. Paca Street, Baltimore, Md. 21201
(410) 685-3063

**History
of the
Shrine:**

St. Jude Parish was entrusted to the Pallottines by the archbishop of
Baltimore in 1917. Around the outset of World War II, devotion to St.
Jude was reaching meaningful proportions in the parish, and so it was
decided that a shrine should be established in his honor and that novena
services should be scheduled on a regular basis.

Interest in the shrine and the services grew so rapidly that it became
necessary to initiate mailings in order to answer inquiries and to respond
to requests regarding the offering of Masses of petitions and/or
thanksgiving to St. Jude. Mailings extended beyond the boundaries of
the State of Maryland in 1953.

To keep pace with the growing demand of the devotees of St. Jude,
three solemn novenas throughout the year were instituted as were
regular weekly services.

Pallottine priests and brothers offer daily prayers in response to the
many requests and petitions received. It is always of great interest to the
Pallottines, in line with the furtherance of the devotion to St. Jude, to
know of the many favors that have been received through his
intercession.

The Pallottine priests and brothers who labor at the shrine respond to the
many letters and calls received from devotees of St. Jude and conduct
the various novenas and other religious services at the shrine.

Today St. Jude's body rests in a tomb in the Vatican Basilica of St.
Peter's. This Baltimore shrine has arranged to have a daily Mass
celebrated on the altar above the tomb for the intentions of those whose
names are registered at the shrine.

**Schedule
of Masses:**

Sunday: 8:00 a.m., 9:00 a.m., and 11:30 a.m.
Daily: 7:00 a.m., 12:05 p.m.
Saturday: 7:45 a.m.
Confessions: Fifteen minutes before all services

Devotions:

Novenas to St. Jude
Novena services: Sunday: Following the 9:00 a.m. and 11:30 a.m.
Masses; Wednesday: 7:45 a.m. (Novena and Mass); 12:00 p.m. (Novena
and Mass); 5:45 p.m. (Novena and Benediction); and 7:45 p.m. (Novena
and Benediction)

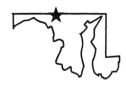

NATIONAL SHRINE GROTTO OF LOURDES

Mount St. Mary's College, Emmitsburg, Md. 21727
(301) 447-6122

History of the Shrine:

Above the lovely valley of Emmitsburg, Md., situated high on a mountainside overlooking Mount St. Mary's campus and the Shrine of St. Elizabeth Ann Seton, a statue of Our Lady rises atop the Pangborn Memorial Campanile.

Fr. John DuBois, a refugee priest from France, came to the Emmitsburg area. The priest, who later became the third bishop of New York, was appointed pastor of Frederick by Bishop Carroll. Fr. DuBois found the grotto site, in a small wooded valley, of breathtaking beauty. He also found a natural amphitheater where nature "displayed itself in all its wild and picturesque beauty."

A great statue of the Blessed Mother presides over the Valley of St. Mary from her mountain. The melody of the bells, ringing out the Angelus and sacred hymns, call all minds and hearts to Jesus through Mary. Fr. DuBois built his church on this lofty site in order that the people in the valley, during their daily tasks, would look up, would see the cross and their Blessed Mother and would "keep the faith." This campanile perpetuates the holy purpose of the founder.

In addition to the campanile and grotto lie an exquisite rosary walk and the Stations of the Cross. Well over one million pilgrims journey to the grotto each year to refresh their souls and to enliven their faith in God.

It has been said of Lourdes that, even though Our Lady never appeared there, it would be worth a trip from the other side of the world just to see the natural beauty of the spot. The same is true of the mountain grotto.

Schedule of Masses:

Sunday: 12:00 p.m. and 5:00 p.m.

Devotions:

Novena to Our Lady of Lourdes: Sunday: 3:00 p.m., with a homily and benediction.
Anointing of the Sick: After all services at the grotto.
Ecumenical Easter Sunday Sunrise Service: 6:30 a.m., followed by Mass at 7:30 a.m. (This event attracts people of all faiths.)
Medjugorje Day: May 25
Seventy-fifth Anniversary of Our Lady of Fatima: July 20-21
Annual Novena to Our Lady of the Assumption: August 7-15
Feast of Our Lady of the Assumption: Solemn Mass with a special speaker each year on August 15
Feast of the Holy Angels: October 2

NATIONAL SHRINE OF ST. ELIZABETH ANN SETON

333 South Seton Avenue, Emmitsburg, Md. 21727
(301) 447-6606

**History
of the
Shrine:**

Mother Seton and her companions arrived in Emmitsburg, Md., on June 24, 1809, and moved into the stone house about a month later. In February 1810, she and her companions moved into what is known today as the White House. On the twentieth of that month, the Blessed Sacrament was carried in procession from the stone house to St. Joseph's House by the Rev. John Dubois. The chapel was completed in March, and the first high Mass within its walls was celebrated on the Feast of St. Joseph. A school opened here by Mother Seton for the children of the neighborhood was the first parochial school in the United States.

On January 4, 1821, Mother Seton died in the room adjoining the chapel. She was buried under a great oak tree until the completion of the Mortuary Chapel in 1846. During that year, her remains were placed in a vault beneath the floor of the chapel where they rested until their exhumation in 1962 prior to her beatification by Pope John XXIII in 1963.

In 1968, the relics of Elizabeth Ann Seton were transferred to the newly erected Seton Shrine Chapel of St. Joseph's Provincial House of the Daughters of Charity. Pope Paul VI canonized this first daughter of the United States of America on September 14, 1975. On August 28, 1976, the chapel was solemnly dedicated as the St. Elizabeth Ann Seton Chapel by the Most Rev. William D. Borders, archbishop of Baltimore.

A visit to the Shrine of St. Elizabeth Ann Seton calls attention not only to her heroic life of charity, but also to the deeper reality that God was with her, that her daily spiritual life brought her into loving touch with her God. The shrine center and historic buildings are open daily except for Christmas Day, the last two weeks of January, and Mondays from November 1 to April 1.

**Schedule
of Masses:**

Saturday and Sunday: 9:00 a.m.
Wednesday-Sunday: 1:30 p.m., followed by the blessing with the relic of St. Elizabeth Ann Seton
Confessions: After the 1:30 p.m. liturgy and upon request

Devotions: Novena: Daily to St. Elizabeth Ann Seton

Facilities: Gift Shop

BASILICA OF ST. MARY OF THE IMMACULATE CONCEPTION

232 Chapel Street, Norfolk, Va, 23504 (804) 622-4487

History of the Shrine:

The Basilica of St. Mary of the Immaculate Conception, located in downtown Norfolk, is the oldest parish community in the Catholic Diocese of Richmond and is often referred to as "The Mother Church of Tidewater Virginia."

The church came into existence in 1791 as St. Patrick's Church, two years before the establishment of the U.S. hierarchy and twenty-nine years before the institution of the Richmond diocese. Its first parishioners were French Catholics, compelled to abandon their native land by the French Revolution. St. Patrick's received some of the earliest Irish Catholic immigrants in the United States.

The original church was built in 1842 but was destroyed by fire in 1856, rendering the building unusable as a church. In 1858, the present church building was erected. It was dedicated to Mary of the Immaculate Conception and was the first church to bear the name after the promulgation of the dogma of the Immaculate Conception by Pope Pius IX.

African American Catholics began attending St. Mary's in 1886 where a portion of the choir loft was reserved for them. Subsequently, in 1889 the Josephites began coming from Richmond and by September of that year, St. Joseph's Black Catholic parish was founded with the Josephites serving as priests. Their mission was to serve the spiritual needs of the Black community. Seventy-two years later, in 1961, St. Joseph's was merged with St. Mary's. On November 1, 1981, the newly renovated/restored edifice was rededicated with the Most Rev. Pio Laghi, apostolic pro-nuncio, the principal celebrant.

Today, St. Mary's Catholic Church is 99 percent African-American. The parish supports St. Mary's Academy, an inner-city school that provides a Christian education to hundreds of urban children, most of whom are non-Catholic. The parish also operates a soup kitchen and provides other outreach to Norfolk's poor and homeless.

On December 8, 1991, the Church of St. Mary of the Immaculate Conception became a Minor Basilica, which coincided with the two hundredth anniversary of the church. The official proclamation was read by Apostolic Pro-Nuncio, Archbishop Agostino Cacciavillan, the principal celebrant of the Liturgy. The Basilica is an honorary title recognizing the distinguished nature of St. Mary's. There are thirty-three other minor basilicas in the United States, with St. Mary's being the only one in the Commonwealth of Virginia. December 8 is the main celebration at the Basilica.

**Schedule
of Masses:**   Sunday Vigil: 6:00 p.m.
Sunday: 9:00 a.m. and 12:00 p.m.
Daily: Tuesday-Friday: 12:10 p.m.
Holy Day of Obligation: 12:10 p.m. and 7:30 p.m.
Confessions: Saturday: 5:30 p.m. and upon request

Devotions: Rosary: Before Sunday Masses
Christian Initiation Program for Adults: Weekly
Christian Initiation Program for Children: Weekly
Feast of the Immaculate Conception: December 8

Facilities: Soup Kitchen
St. Mary's Academy: Pre-K through Fifth Grade

Languages: English and North American Sign Language

WEST

SHRINE OF ST. THERESE

5933 Lund Street, Juneau, Alaska 99801 (907) 780-6112

**History
of the
Shrine:**

Fr. William G. LeVasseur, SJ, had a vision of establishing a retreat center/shrine on an island along the Inside Passage, a Pacific Ocean waterway amid forested islands. With the blessing and support of Bishop Joseph Raphael Crimont, the dream began to take shape during the 1930s. With much volunteer help and through the grace of God, a stone chapel, a log retreat lodge, and smaller retreat cabins were constructed near the shrine.

The shrine was dedicated to St. Therese of Lisieux, who was chosen to be the patroness of Alaska by Bishop Crimont, the first bishop for the entire state of Alaska. St. Therese is a twentieth-century saint known for the little ways in which she reached out to God's people as a way to please her Creator and Lord. She believed that the God of Mercy had a special love for ordinary people because he created so many of them, and she considered herself among them. The message of St. Therese teaches us that no one has to earn God's love; he loves us first, and our call is to respond to and accept that love and in turn share that love.

The chapel, lodge, and cabins serve the needs of those on retreats and also provide a place of spiritual refuge and renewal for individuals, couples, families, and groups.

**Schedule
of Masses:**

Sunday: 1:00 p.m. (Summer)
Confessions: Upon request

Devotions:

Memorial Day: Annually
Corpus Christi: Annually
Feast of St. Therese of Lisieux: Annually
Bishop Crimont's Anniversary: Annually
Retreats: Monthly
Day of Recollection: Varies

Facilities:

Retreat Lodge Center with overnight accommodations
Other overnight accommodations (e.g., cabins available for small retreats)
Religious Gift Shop
Cafeteria (meals are provided with lodge retreats)
Shrine: services, weddings

**Other
Activities:**

Fishing
Picnicking
Beachcombing
Outdoor Stations of the Cross

SHRINE OF ST. JOSEPH OF THE MOUNTAINS

P.O. Box 1027, Yarnell, Ariz. 85362 (602) 427-3339
(602) 427-3629 or 841-8741

History of the Shrine:

The Shrine of St. Joseph of the Mountains was conceived during the Great Depression as a symbol of reassurance, personified by Joseph, head of the Holy Family. The shrine was established in the late 1930s by the Catholic Action League. A statue of St. Joseph stands at the base of a winding, ascending stone stairway, greeting visitors who come for undistracted contemplation of the redemption symbolized by the life of Christ.

William and Mary Wasson, who donated the land, belonged to the Catholic Action League, a volunteer group organized in the 1930s to aid the poor. William and Mary dedicated themselves to charity by housing many homeless people under their own roof. In 1937, the Wassons and other league members decided to build a retreat away from the urban trauma of the Depression. Because Joseph was a working man, he was chosen as a symbol with whom all classes could identify.

The shrine contains life-size figures of St. Joseph with the Christ Child; Christ at the Last Supper; The Agony in the Garden; The Crucifixion; Sorrowful Mother; The Tomb; and the Risen Christ. The Stations of the Cross wind their way up and around the beautiful surrounding hills.

The shrine began during a time of need. Then it became a war memorial. Now it has returned to its original emphasis: charity.

Schedule of Masses: Periodic Masses

Devotions: La Posada
Stations and Easter Services, when priest is available

Facilities: Gift Shop

Languages: English and Spanish, when priest is available

BASILICA OF SAN CARLOS BORROMEO

(Carmel Mission) Rio Road and Lausen Drive,
P.O. Box 2235, Carmel, Calif. 93921 (408) 624-1271

**History
of the
Shrine:**

Carmel Mission stands today as a monument to Padre Junípero Serra, who left his home to come to our western wilderness in order to preach the Gospel of Christ. Padre Serra arrived by vessel at Monterey, Calif., on June 3, 1770, and founded the Mission of San Carlos. On August 24, 1771, with few provisions, he took up his abode at Carmel and began his ministry there. Padre Serra also founded nine other missions. His frail health overtook him at age seventy-one, and he died on August 28, 1784, leaving behind a thriving mission. From 1770 to 1836, over four thousand Native Americans were baptized at Carmel.

The mission was then run by Padre Lausen who in 1793 undertook the building of the present stone church, which had been the hope of Padre Serra. Over the next four years, the church was built on the site of the first adobe church, from the native sandstone quarried from the nearby Santa Lucia Mountains. The church was dedicated in 1797.

By 1823 the Indian population had dwindled and, eleven years later, Carmel was secularized. Destruction of the mission life was complete by 1836. The church gradually went into decay and ruin, and it was not until 1884 that Fr. Casanova began the work of saving this historic landmark. A new era of building began in 1931, and two years later, Bishop Scher of the diocese raised Carmel Mission to the status of parish church.

In 1960, Pope John XXIII, through the Sacred Congregation of Rites, granted Bishop Willinger's petition that Carmel Mission as a historical shrine be raised to the status of minor basilica. It now stands as one of the few basilicas of the western United States.

The mission church, two museums, cemetery, and Munras Memorial are open to the public.

**Schedule
of Masses:**

Sunday: 7:00 a.m., 8:00 a.m., 9:30 a.m., 11:00 a.m., 12:30 p.m., and 5:30 p.m.
Daily: 7:00 a.m., 12:00 p.m., and 5:30 p.m.

Devotions:

Vespers: First Friday: 7:30 p.m.

SHRINE OF OUR LADY OF SORROWS

745 Ware Avenue, Colusa, Calif. 95932
(916) 458-4170

**History
of the
Shrine:**

The shrine is the site of the first Catholic Mass celebrated in Colusa County, Calif., by Fr. Peter Magagnotto, a Passionist priest from Marysville. In 1864, a German missionary, Fr. Lefauber, conducted a mission at the site. As a memorial of the mission, he erected a cross, 27-feet high with a crosspiece 12-feet long.

The idea of building a church here was abandoned in favor of establishing a church in Colusa. However, Masses, pilgrimages, and visits continued at the site, which became the property of the Diocese of Sacramento in 1883.

Later in 1883, Fr. Michael Wallrath, of the church in Colusa, erected a small shrine containing an altar within a few feet of the wooden cross. He dedicated the shrine to Our Lady of Sorrows. In 1922, the shrine was restored by the Knights of Columbus, and the rotted wooden cross was replaced by a large white cement cross.

The shrine was placed on the National Register of Historic Places in December 1974, the first landmark in Colusa County to bear that distinction. In 1979, the shrine was again restored, this time by members of the Colusa parish. The altar was painted, the crucifix was restored, and an alms box was placed on the wall. The Ten Commandments were hand lettered on slabs of cement, and a bronze plaque was erected at the entrance of the shrine.

It is hoped that visitors will take time to rest, pray, and meditate, and to attend the annual May Mass.

**Schedule
of Masses:**

One Sunday in May (depending on the weather): 4:00 p.m. The Mass is followed by a picnic supper.

CATHEDRAL OF THE BLESSED SACRAMENT

1017 11th Street, Sacramento, Calif. 85814-3806
(916) 444-3071

History of the Shrine:

The dedication of the Cathedral of the Blessed Sacrament on June 30, 1889, was a momentous event that marked the beginning of its first century as part of the life and witness of the Diocese of Sacramento. The Cathedral's most striking feature was its European stained-glass windows. Made in Austria, the windows incorporate even older glass believed to have been made in the fifteenth century. The renovation of the cathedral's interior in 1971 added the rose window in the balcony and several other panels over the main doors and altar.

The cathedral bells are of special interest. One group of four, the chimes, which are rung to designate the quarter hours, weigh from 1,000 to 4,000 pounds each. The largest bell, which tolls the hour and weighs 8,000 pounds, was a gift of Bishop Manogue. The bell carries an inscription in Latin, which translates as "Morning, noon, and evening we will sing the Praise of the Lord, of the Most Blessed Sacrament, and of St. Patrick."

There are many impressive examples of paintings in the church, the most notable being a reproduction of the *Sistine Madonna* by Raphael Sazio (1488-1520). This reproduction was made possible through diplomatic channels with the King of Saxony, who gave his permission in a letter dated February 10, 1889. Other paintings in the Cathedral include: *The Archangel Michael Crushing Satan, The Holy Family, The Death of a Martyr, The Descent from the Cross, The Stations of the Cross,* and *Our Lady of Guadalupe.*

The Cathedral also includes statues of the Blessed Virgin, St. Joseph, St. Patrick, the Sacred Heart of Jesus, St. Therese of Lisieux, St. Anthony, St. Jude, St. Martín de Porres, and the Infant Jesus of Prague.

The Cathedral of the Blessed Sacrament is the mother church of the Diocese of Sacramento. Visitors of all faiths are welcome to drop in to see the church, to stop and meditate in quiet surroundings, and, if so inclined, to attend one of the services. Tours can be arranged by calling the rectory secretary for an appointment.

Schedule of Masses:

Sunday Vigil: 5:10 p.m.
Sunday: 8:00 a.m., 10:00 a.m., 12:00 p.m., 1:30 p.m. (Spanish), and 5:10 p.m.
Daily: 7:00 a.m., 12:00 p.m., and 5:10 p.m.

Saturday: 12:00 p.m.
Confessions: Monday-Friday: 11:30 a.m.-12:00 p.m.; Saturday: 4:30-5:10 p.m.

Devotions: October: Blessing of animals in honor of St. Francis of Assisi
March: St. Patrick, the patron saint of the diocese

MISSION BASILICA
SAN DIEGO DE ALCALA

10818 San Diego Mission Road, San Diego, Calif.
92108-2498 (619) 283-7319

**History
of the
Shrine:**

The Mission San Diego de Alcala was California's first church, founded on July 16, 1769 by Padre Junípero Serra. The mission was relocated on the site in 1774 in order to be nearer to the Indian villages, a reliable source of water, and good land for farming.

Mission San Diego became known as the Mother of the Missions that stretch through northern California. In 1775, the mission was attacked by Indians who destroyed it by burning the tinder-dry buildings. Padre Luis Jayme was killed in this attack when he tried to calm the Indians; he became the first Christian martyr in California and is buried in the mission sanctuary.

Padre Serra returned to the site in 1776 and began reconstruction of the church and mission buildings. This time, the padres used adobe to cover the walls and tile for the roofs, which would protect them from fire in case of any future attacks. By 1780 most of the reconstruction of the mission and outbuildings was completed. The church and other buildings were arranged in a quadrangle around a patio.

In 1797, 565 Indians received baptism, which brought the number of converts to 1,405. The land area grew to 50,000 acres on which wheat, barley, corn, and beans were cultivated, as well as vineyards, orchards, and a variety of vegetable gardens. During this time, the mission owned 20,000 sheep, 10,000 cattle, and 1,250 horses. The second church was damaged by an earthquake in 1803; the present church has a buttress-like structure which has withstood subsequent earthquakes.

The mission was occupied by the U.S. Calvary during the years 1846-1862. The soldiers made some temporary repairs to the decayed buildings in order to make them habitable. In 1862 the mission lands were restored to the church by order of President Abraham Lincoln.

The present mission church was named a minor basilica by Pope Paul VI in 1976. It serves today as an active parish for the Catholic community and as a cultural center for people of all faiths, who are most welcome to visit the mission and relive the grandeur and excitement of two hundred years.

**Schedule
of Masses:**

Sunday Vigil: 5:30 p.m.
Sunday: 7:00 a.m., 8:00 a.m., and 9:00 a.m. (Folk Mass),10:00 a.m., 11:00 a.m. (Spanish), 12:00 p.m. (Choir), and 5:30 p.m. (Folk Mass)
Daily: 7:00 a.m. and 5:30 p.m.

LA MISION DE
SAN FRANCISCO DE ASIS

3321 16th Street, San Francisco, Calif. 94114
(415) 621-8203

History of the Shrine: The shrine was the sixth of the twenty-one Spanish California missions, founded June 29, 1776 by Fr. Francisco Paulou, OFM, under the direction of Fr. Junípero Serra, O.F.M. It is considered the birthplace of the City of San Francisco and the mother church of northern California. Originally the site of the evangelization of the Costanoan Indians, along with the Basilica it presently serves as a parish church continuing the evangelization work of the Franciscan Missionaries. It provides spiritual life to seventeen hundred families within the territorial boundaries of the parish and to its many visitors from the city and around the world. The larger church, built in 1913, was declared a basilica by Pope Pius XII in 1952.

Important events during the year include *Señor de los Milagros* in October (Peruvian), *La Purisima Concepción* in December (Nicaraguan), *Nuestra Señora de Guadalupe* in December (Mexican), and *Procesión del Santo Entierro* on Good Friday (Hispanic). The founding of the mission is celebrated annually on June 29.

Schedule of Masses: Sunday Vigil: 5:00 p.m.
Sunday: 8:00 a.m., 10:00 a.m., and 12:00 p.m. (Spanish)
Confessions: Saturday: 4:00-5:00 p.m.
Holy Day of Obligation: 7:30 a.m., 9:00 a.m., and 6:00 p.m. (Bilingual)

Devotions: Rosary: Monday-Saturday: 8:40 a.m.
Adoration/Benediction: Friday

Facilities: Old Mission Dolores
Gift Shop
Museum
Cemetery
Basilica

Languages: English and Spanish spoken
English, Spanish, German, and French Old Mission informational brochures

SAN JUAN BAUTISTA MISSION

P.O. Box 410, 2nd and Mariposa Streets, San Juan Bautista, Calif. 95045 (408) 623-2127

History of the Shrine:

San Juan Bautista Mission was founded in 1797 by Fr. Fermin Francisco Lausen, a Franciscan from Vitoria, Spain. It was the fifteenth mission in California and one of the nine started by Fr. Lausen. It is the largest mission and the only one that always had a priest to minister to the Indians and others who came to the West. The mission survived the 1906 earthquake, despite the fact that under the structure runs the famous San Andreas fault.

The mission fiesta, *Dia de San Juan,* is celebrated annually. *Teatro Campesino* is held in December, and Apparitions of Our Lady of Guadalupe and La Pastorella are held every other year.

Schedule of Masses:

Sunday Vigil: 5:30 p.m.
Sunday: 9:00 a.m., 11:00 a.m., and 1:00 p.m. (Spanish)
Confessions: Saturday: 4:00-5:00 p.m. and before Sunday Masses
Holy Day of Obligation Vigil: 5:30 p.m.
Holy Day of Obligation: 8:30 a.m. and 5:30 p.m.

Devotions:

Bible Class: Weekly

Facilities:

Religious Bookstore
Gift Shop
Picnic Grounds

Languages:

English, Spanish, Portuguese, and Italian

MISSION SAN LUIS REY

4050 Mission Avenue, San Luis Rey, Calif. 92068
(619) 757-3651

**History
of the
Shrine:**

Mission San Luis Rey, established in 1798, is the eighteenth of the twenty-one California missions, founded by the Franciscans in the eighteenth and early nineteenth centuries. In 1865, at the end of the Period of Secularization (when missions were auctioned off by the Mexican government), President Lincoln signed a congressional bill requiring all missions to be returned to the church in California. Reconstruction and restoration of the mission began in 1892, and today the mission is a thriving parish, tourist attraction, and retreat center.

A fiesta is celebrated on the third weekend in July, and the Heritage Ball is held on the second Saturday of September. Approximately fifty thousand people visit the mission annually.

**Schedule
of Masses:**

Sunday Vigil: 5:30 p.m.
Sunday: 6:30 a.m., 7:30 a.m., 9:00 a.m., 10:30 a.m., 12:00 p.m., and 7:30 p.m.
Confessions: Saturday: 4:00-5:00 p.m.

Devotions:

Retreats: Weekly
Family Spiritual Vacation

Facilities:

Religious Bookstore
Overnight Accommodations
Gift Shop

Languages:

English and Spanish

SHRINE OF OUR LADY OF PEACE

2800 Mission College Boulevard, Santa Clara, Calif. 95054
(408) 988-4585

History of the Shrine:

In 1976 Fr. John Sweeney, pastor of Our Lady of Peace Church in Santa Clara, Calif., commissioned noted sculptor Charles Parks to portray through the medium of stainless steel a statue of the Blessed Virgin Mary.

Begun in 1980, the 7,200-pound statue rises to a height of 32 feet and rests on a 12-foot landscaped mound. The head, hands, and feet are cast in stainless steel. The gown is constructed of welded strips of stainless steel.

The Shrine of Our Lady of Peace was dedicated on October 7, 1983, by Most Rev. Pierre DuMaine, bishop of San Jose. A hand-illumined papal blessing was presented to the shrine on that occasion.

The Shrine of Our Lady of Peace holds a Fatima Pilgrimage on the thirteenth day of each month, May through October, with Mass beginning at 7:30 p.m. In 1917, Mary appeared to three children in Fatima, Portugal, on those days and invited all the world to pray for peace. This pilgrimage reproduces the identical ceremonies celebrated at Fatima with a candlelight rosary and blessing of the sick.

Schedule of Masses:

Sunday Vigil: 5:00 p.m.
Sunday: 7:30 a.m., 9:00 a.m., 10:30 a.m., 12:00 p.m., 5:00 p.m., and 7:00 p.m.
Holy Day of Obligation Vigil: 7:30 p.m.
Holy Day of Obligation: 8:00 a.m., 9:00 a.m., 12:00 p.m., 5:15 p.m., and 7:30 p.m.
Daily: 8:00 a.m., 12:00 p.m., and 5:15 p.m.; also Wednesday: 7:30 p.m., and Saturday: 8:00 a.m.
First Friday: 8:00 a.m., 12:00 p.m., 5:15 p.m., and 7:30 p.m.
Confessions: Saturday: 3:30-5:00 p.m. and 7:30-9:00 p.m., as well as before all Masses and upon request.

Devotions:

Tuesday: 11:00 a.m. Holy Hour and celebration of the Eucharist in honor of Mary
First Friday: All-night vigil beginning with Mass at 7:30 p.m. and concluding with First Saturday Mass at 5:00 a.m.
Fatima Pilgrimage: Thirteenth day of each month. Mass at 7:30 p.m.
Perpetual Adoration: The Blessed Sacrament is exposed day and night for perpetual adoration.

SAN BUENAVENTURA MISSION

211 East Main Street, Ventura, Calif. 93001
(805) 643-4318

History of the Shrine:

Fr. Junípero Serra raised a cross at *la playa de la canal de Santa Barbara*, the beach of the Santa Barbara Channel, on Easter morning, March 31, 1782. Assisted by Padre Pedro Benito Cambon, he celebrated a High Mass and dedicated a mission to San Buenaventura (St. Bonaventure).

Following the mission's first church building's destruction by fire, the construction of a second church was abandoned because "the door gave way." In 1792, work began on the present church and the small utility building, which formed a quadrangle enclosing a plaza. The church was completed in 1809 and was dedicated on September 9, 1809; the first liturgical services took place a day later.

In December 1976, the church was solemnly consecrated by Timothy Cardinal Manning. Six years later, the mission marked its bicentennial anniversary. The old mission welcomes visitors and pilgrims anytime.

Schedule of Masses:

Sunday Vigil: 5:30 p.m. and 7:30 p.m. (Spanish)
Sunday: 7:30 a.m., 9:00 a.m., 10:30 a.m. (Spanish), and 12:00 p.m.
Holy Day of Obligation Vigil: 5:30 p.m.
Holy Day of Obligation: 7:30 a.m., 12:00 p.m., 5:30 p.m., and 7:30 p.m. (Spanish)
Daily: 7:30 a.m.
Confessions: Saturday: 3:30-5:00 p.m.; also Monday after Novena Mass.

Devotions:

Mass and Novena to Our Lady of the Miraculous Medal: Monday: 7:30 p.m.
The rosary is recited daily.

Facilities:

Gift Shop
Religious Bookstore
Mission Museum

Languages:

English and Spanish

MOTHER CABRINI SHRINE

20189 Cabrini Boulevard, Golden, Colo. 80401
(303) 526-0758

**History
of the
Shrine:**

This shrine was established by St. Frances Xavier Cabrini for the purpose of spreading the gospel and of providing a peaceful summer atmosphere for orphan children.

On the site of the shrine lie large white stones that Mother Cabrini arranged in the shape of a heart, surrounded by a smaller stone cross and a crown of thorns. A 22-foot statue of the Sacred Heart stands adorned by the Stations of the Cross, the Mysteries of the Rosary, and the Ten Commandments. A cool spring of miraculous water still flows today after Mother Cabrini found it on the barren hilltop. The main celebration of the year is the annual pilgrimage in July, which always attracts a large crowd.

The Missionary Sisters of the Sacred Heart of Jesus, founded by St. Cabrini, serve and minister to the needs of the many people who visit the shrine daily, seeking comfort, solace, and the Lord's peace.

**Schedule
of Masses:**

Sunday: 7:30 a.m. and 11:00 a.m.
Holy Day of Obligation: 7:30 a.m.
Confessions: prior to Sunday Masses

Devotions:

Novenas: Annually
Retreats: Annually

Facilities:

Overnight Accommodations
Gift Shop
Cafeteria
Museum

Languages:

English and Spanish

THE SHRINE OF THE STATIONS OF THE CROSS (SANGRE DE CRISTO)

P.O. Box 326, 511 Church Place, San Luis, Colo. 81152
(719) 672-3685

History of the Shrine:

The Sangre de Cristo was built as an act of faith and love by the parishioners of the Sangre de Cristo Parish. It was conceived in 1986, the centennial jubilee year of the parish.

The Shrine of the Stations of the Cross is located on a mesa in the center of San Luis, Colorado's oldest town. The shrine is known formally as *"La Mesa de la Piedad y de la Misericordia"* ("Hill of Piety and Mercy").

The Stations of the Cross are a series of graphic meditations of the last hours of Christ's life, his judgment, sufferings, and death. Christ's Resurrection is symbolized as the "15th" Station.

The trail, which is less than a mile long, culminates in a Grotto of Our Lady of Guadalupe that contains pink sandstone statues of Juan Diego and the Virgin carved in Mexico. The grotto is a reminder of the special place that Mary has in the role of salvation and of the love that Hispanics have for the Mother of God under the title of Our Lady of Guadalupe.

Schedule of Masses:

Sunday Vigil: 7:00 p.m.
Sunday: 10:00 a.m.
Daily: 7:00 a.m.
Holy Day of Obligation Vigil: 7:00 p.m.
Holy Day of Obligation: 10:00 a.m.

Devotions:

Novena to San Isidro: Nine days before May 15
Feast of San Isidro: May 15
Feast of San Acasio: June 15
Feast of Ss. Peter and Paul: June 28 and 29
Feast of St. James: July 25
Feast of St. Ann: July 26

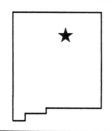

EL SANTUARIO DE CHIMAYO

The Shrine of Our Lord of Esquipulas
P.O. Box 235, Chimayo, N.Mex. 87522 (505) 351-4889 or
(505) 351-4360

**History
of the
Shrine:**

El Santuario was built between 1814 and 1816. The miraculous crucifix of Our Lord of Esquipulas was founded about 1810. There is no written testimony concerning the apparition of Our Lord in the Chimayo area. Tradition has passed down the story from one generation to another by the people of El Potrero.

El Santuario has been called the Lourdes of America, although no one seems to know exactly how the name came about. There are testimonies that miracles have occurred. Fr. Sebastian Alvarez, in his letter to the Episcopal See of Durango, dated November 16, 1813, told of the people coming from afar to seek cure for their ailments. As word spread about these cures, many more faithful came in pilgrimage. El Santuario became a place of worship — a place to pray, to thank, to ask, to meditate, and to experience peace of mind and body.

The mass media began to notice the little shrine in the Sangre de Cristo mountains. Newspapers from Chicago, Denver, New York, and Los Angeles and *Time* and *Newsweek* magazines have all written about the shrine, resulting in a considerable number of requests for information about the shrine. Thousands of people come to El Santuario, close to 300,000 annually, to worship the Almighty, to ask for peace, to fulfill a promise, and to feel the healing touch of God.

The shrine is open to visitors daily from 9:00 a.m.-5:00 p.m., June through September, and from 9:00 a.m.-4:00 p.m., October through May.

**Schedule
of Masses:**

Sunday: 12:00 p.m.
Daily: 7:00 a.m. (October-May); 11:00 a.m. (June-September)

Facilities:

Gift Shop

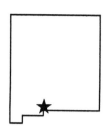

SHRINE AND PARISH OF OUR LADY OF GUADALUPE

P.O. Box 296, 3600 Parroquia St., Mesilla Park, N.Mex. 88047 (505) 526-8171

History of the Shrine: Descendants of Tigua and Piro Indians, who had settled in this area in 1849, held an annual fiesta and dances in honor of Our Lady of Guadalupe in the city of Las Cruces, N.Mex., until the year 1910, when they were refused permission to continue their cultural practices. This led the Indians to build a small chapel on their own lands to the south of Las Cruces.

In 1914, the chapel and surrounding land were deeded to the Catholic Church with the condition that the Indians would be permitted their cultural practices and annual fiesta in honor of Our Lady of Guadalupe. In 1917, a resident priest was assigned to the pueblo, and the shrine was given parochial status. In 1921, the present adobe church was completed as an enlargement of the original chapel.

The annual fiesta begins on the evening of December 10 with a night watch (*velorio*); December 11 is a day of pilgrimage to *Tortugas* mountain; December 12 is observed with Mass and Indian dances at the shrine, rosary, and benediction of the Blessed Sacrament and a procession through the streets of the village.

The public is invited to take part in all activities December 10-12.

Schedule of Masses: Sunday Vigil: 6:30 p.m.
Sunday: 7:30 a.m. (English), 9:00 a.m. (Spanish), 10:30 a.m. (English)
Holy Day of Obligation: 8:00 a.m. and 6:30 p.m.
Confessions: Saturday: 4:00 p.m. and 7:15 p.m. and upon request

Devotions: Rosary: Twelfth of each month at *La Capilla*
Palm Sunday: Blessing of *ramos*
Feast of St. John: Sunday nearest June 24

Facilities: Indian dining room serves free meals from 12:00-3:00 p.m. on December 12

Languages: English and Spanish

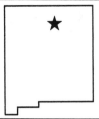

OUR LADY OF THE ROSARY SHRINE

St. Francis Cathedral, The Lady Chapel of the Cathedral, Santa Fe, N.Mex. 87501 (505) 982-5619

History of the Shrine:

The shrine is located in Santa Fe, the oldest capital city in the United States. On January 24, 1625, a Hispanic community in Santa Fe received a statue of Our Lady of the Rosary carved in Spain in the sixteenth century. The statue, hand-carved of willow wood and standing 28 inches tall, became an object of admiration to the Spanish colonists and Indians visiting Santa Fe and was called *La Conquistadora,* Our Lady of Conquering Love of All.

During the Indian rebellion in 1680, the statue was taken by the colonists to El Paso de Norte. In 1693, it was returned to Santa Fe by Don Diego de Vargas, who made a solemn vow of eternal remembrance, after the peaceful reconquest of Santa Fe from the Indians. In 1694, the colonists began an annual thanksgiving observance by taking *La Conquistadora* from her parish shrine to the encampment site where they had prayed to her for victory. The statue is still carried in procession annually through the streets of Santa Fe to Rosario Chapel. It then remains at the chapel for one week, at which time Novena Masses are offered daily.

The papal coronation of the image was ordered by Pope John XXIII in 1960. For over 366 years, Our Lady has helped the families in the area to preserve their faith through active confraternity. The confraternity unites thousands of descendants of the Christians of Santa Fe and New Mexico. *La Cofradia,* as it is called in Spanish, celebrates fifty-five Marian Masses and feasts in the Hispanic Catholic tradition.

The main celebrations of the year are the Double Sunday Processions and Double Novena of Masses of Thanksgiving to Our Lady. The shrine is staffed by the Franciscan Order.

Schedule of Masses:

Sunday Vigil: 5:15 p.m.
Sunday: 6:00 a.m., 8:00 a.m. (Spanish), 10:00 a.m., 12:00 p.m., and 7:00 p.m.
Confessions: Monday-Saturday: 3:00-5:00 p.m.
Holy Day of Obligation Masses follow Sunday schedule.

Devotions: Novenas: Annually (Sunday after Corpus Christi)

Languages: English and Spanish and Indian languages

NATIONAL SANCTUARY OF OUR SORROWFUL MOTHER — THE GROTTO

85th and N.E. Sandy Boulevard, P.O. Box 20008
Portland, Oreg. 97220

History of the Shrine:

The shrine was founded by Rev. Ambrose M. Mayer, OSM, of Kitchenor, Ontario, Canada, as an act of gratitude to God for an answer to a prayer for his mother. She was close to death as a result of childbirth. Fr. Mayer, a boy at the time, promised to do something great for God if she were allowed to live.

Fr. Mayer was sent to Portland in later years as a Servite priest. With permission from superiors and the bishop of the archdiocese, Fr. Mayer purchased fifty-eight acres of land and established what is today the National Sanctuary of Our Sorrowful Mother. The shrine was dedicated by the Most Rev. Alexander Christie, archbishop of Portland, on July 16, 1925.

Permission was granted by Pope Pius XI on February 8, 1930 to celebrate Mother's Day as a Liturgical Feast (Ecce Mater Tua).

Schedule of Masses:

Sunday: 10:00 a.m. and 12:00 p.m. (outdoors May-October)
Daily: 12:00 p.m.
Saturday: 8:00 a.m.
Holy Day of Obligation: 12:00 p.m.
Confessions: By appointment

Devotions:

St. Peregrine: 12:00 p.m., First Saturday of each month
Freedom Day Celebration sponsored by the Southeast Asian Vicariate, Archdiocese of Portland: July.
Festival of Lights Christmas Celebration

Facilities:

Counseling Center

Alphabetical Listing
of Shrines

(Using Proper Titles)

Shrines and Places
Dedicated to the Mystery of Christ

Shrines and Places
Dedicated to the Blessed Mother

Shrines and Places
Dedicated to the Saints